Kurt Hahn's deep understanding of young [illegible] his immense practicality are particularly ev[illegible] [illegible] Seven Laws of Salem," on which he based his first boarding schools in Germany.

1. Give the children the opportunities for self-discovery.
2. Make the children meet with triumph and defeat.
3. Give the children the opportunity of self-effacement in the common cause.
4. Provide periods of silence.
5. Train the imagination.
6. Make games important but not predominant.
7. Free the sons of the wealthy and powerful from the enervating sense of privilege.

KURT HAHN'S SCHOOLS & LEGACY

To Discover You Can Be More and Do More Than You Believed

THE STORY OF ONE OF THE 20TH CENTURY'S MOST INNOVATIVE AND INSPIRING EDUCATORS

MARTIN FLAVIN

THE MIDDLE ATLANTIC PRESS
Wilmington, Delaware

Manufactured in the United States of America

Library of Congress Catalog Card Number: 96-076542

ISBN: 0-912608-78-1

First printing, October 1996

The Middle Atlantic Press, Inc.
848 Church Street
Wilmington, Delaware 19894

For Tomoko

ACKNOWLEDGMENTS

I am grateful to all those who have read the manuscript and encouraged me by their enthusiasm: Josh Miner, founding trustee of Outward Bound USA; Greg Farrell; Steve Truitt; Dyke Brown, founder of the first US Hahnian boarding school, and M.C.S-R. Pyper, headmaster of Gordonstoun. Jocelin Winthrop-Young and Sophie Weidlich (founder and curator of the Kurt Hahn archive) not only helped me assemble archival material, but have read and corrected some errors in the manuscript, and tracked down some of the old photographs. My editor, Alice Gleason, has helped me to condense and focus the story.

For permission to quote I am especially indebted to David Byatt, Warden at Gordonstoun School, without whose marvelous collection of Hahn anecdotes this book could not have come alive. To Josh Miner I am indebted for extensive quotations from *Outward Bound USA* and for his vivid description of Gordonstoun in Hahn's time. W. W. Norton has granted permission to quote from the late Golo Mann some reminiscences of Salem in the twenties. For the quotations from Hahn's radio talks reprinted in *The Listener*, I have been unable to contact this defunct magazine at its last known address.

CONTENTS

Area of inset

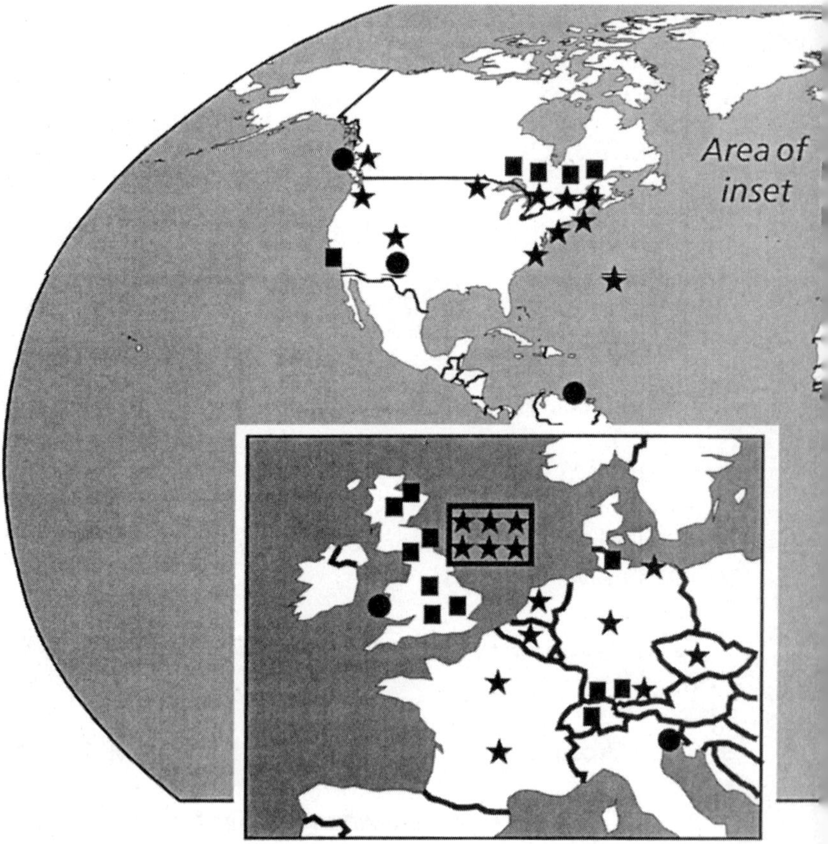

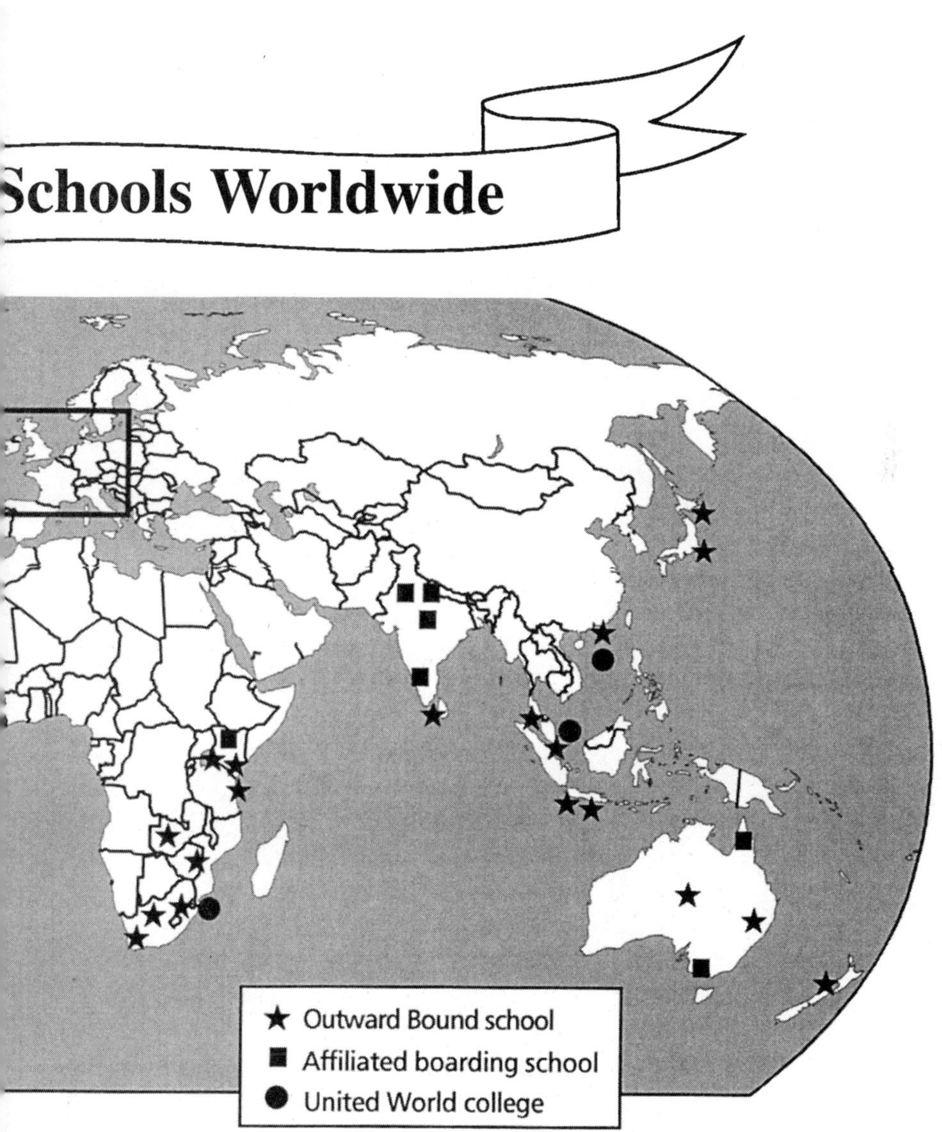

A map showing the approximate location of some of Kurt Hahn's schools today. Prepared by the author and Dan MacDermatt

PREFACE

This book is a memoir of Kurt Hahn, one of the century's most innovative and influential educators and, to my mind, one of its most benevolent public figures. The story begins with his early life in Berlin, and two experiences which exercised a deep influence. One was the admiration he developed for English country boarding schools, both traditional and unconventional, during years of graduate study at Oxford. The second was his behind-the-scenes contact with influential German leaders in World War I who, he discovered, generally lacked the character or civil courage to act upon their convictions. His commmitment to seeking a negotiated peace was shared with the last Imperial Chancellor, Markgraf Max von Baden, and in 1920 he realized a long-standing ambition by opening a country boarding school at the Markgraf's estate at Salem in southern Germany.

Innovations at Salem were not in the classroom, but in the establishment of principles and practices to foster character development and preparation for life. From Pindar he borrowed the principle "Grow into what you are," meaning there is more in you than you think. Hahn accordingly helped students to discover their potentialities by stressing physical fitness for the less adept rather than grooming champions in competitive games, and by granting chosen seniors critical responsibilities essential to the school's survival. Above all, Hahn offered the challenge of adventure in countless forms. The reader will discover, among many principles and practices, an emphasis on the conquest of self-deception, and on the overmastering of selfishness for the benefit of the community.

Arrested and exiled almost immediately after Hitler came to power in January 1933, Hahn founded Gordonstoun school in Scotland. It was during and after his twenty years as director there that he conceived and created a series of institutions that have spread his ideas and principles to vast numbers of young people around the world. Today almost four million boys and girls have participated in, and a greater number has been indirectly influenced by, the Outward Bound Schools and the Award Schemes.

The second part of the book tells the story of the defiant startegies by which Hahn's German schools survived the thirteen years of Nazi rule. Hahn was not there during these years, except in memory, but perhaps this episode still has some place in a memoir of Hahn. It was there, and probably also during the many years before 1920 when he was planning to start the school, that all his basic principles were developed. Now we can see how these principles fared under the worst conceivable circumstances. I was a student at Salem through the first year of the Nazi regime, during part of which Prince Philip (later spouse of the English Monarch) was a schoolmate and friend. Since I kept an extensive diary, we can also see how one thirteen-year-old American boy was impressed by the school and by the Nazis.

At another level, these chapters also provide an honest account of everyday life in a small German community that opposed the Nazi regime. One caution. The assaults which the Nazis made on this every day life were relatively trivial. To any younger reader who may be unfamiliar with the full extent of the Nazi crimes, and who wishes to know more, one place to begin might be Primo Levi's first-hand account, *Survival in Auschwitz*

Kurt Hahn and the Origins of the Salem Schools

In 1933-4 I spent my thirteenth year far away from my home in California, at a coeducational boarding school near the Bodensee (The Lake of Constance) in southern Germany. The founder and director of Salem was not there when I arrived, nor can I find his name mentioned in the diary that I kept, some 300 pages typed every few days on my father's cast-off Corona.

Kurt Hahn had been arrested by the Nazis 6 weeks before my arrival, and only a month after Hitler came to power. Hitler's first anti-semitic decree at this time directed that all Jewish civil servants teaching in the public schools be "retired." But the fact that Hahn was Jewish did not account for his precipitous arrest, only a month after Hitler came to power on January 30 1933, but was prompted by an earlier act of defiance. In August 1932 Hitler had sent a telegram of congratulation to 5 storm-troopers who had been sentenced to death for the murder of a young communist, whom they had arbitrarilly dragged from his bed and fatally trampled to death in the presence of his mother.

Referring to this telegram, Hahn had written [1] to all Salem alumni: "It is a question now in Germany of its Christian civilization, its reputation, its soldierly honour; Salem cannot remain neutral. I call on all members of the Salem association who are active in the SA or the SS to terminate their allegiance either to Hitler or to Salem."

Except for Hitler's telegram the Potempa murder, named after the village where it occurred [2], would have been lost in a profusion of similar violent episodes of the era. Street fighting had become widespread in 1932 as uniformed Nazi storm troopers began an armed assault, which was effectively repulsed, against working-class residential districts, clubs and workers' organizations. As registered unemployment rose in 1932 to 30% (44% among unionized workers), street fighting and membership in various militias became a palliative for emotional stress and loss of self-respect.

After the Potempa murder Hitler telegraphed the convicted storm troopers: "My comrades! In the face of this monstrous death sentence I feel myself bound to you through unlimited loyalty. Your freedom is from this moment a question of our honour. The battle against a regime under which this was possible is our duty." No one today would want to try to specify the earliest moment at which the Nazi's intentions had been revealed, but Hitler's telegram may have seemed then to some to prove that standards of justice would not restrain the Nazis' future actions.

The sentence of the Potempa muderers was soon commuted to life imprisonment by von Papen, and when Hitler came to power they were released under an amnesty, limited to the "champions of the national uprising."

Kurt Hahn's arrest was not unanticipated. As early as 1924 the newspaper Bodensee Rundschau had published an article entitled "Prince Max von Baden and his court Jew" (the school was domiciled at Prince Max's estate), and this pro-Nazi paper reported [3] a week before his arrest that it had seen an "impertinent letter from....the freemason and arch-jew Kurt Hahn, in which he goes so far as to say, in his hatred of Germany, that he will pursue Hitler like a plague."

Kurt Hahn escaped to England in July 1933, and within a year had founded a new school in Scotland, based on the principles of Salem, as will be described in the next chapter. But we should begin by examining some personal and cultural forces which influenced the origins of these principles, and their realization in the Salem schools in Germany.

Kurt Hahn was born in 1886 into a cultivated Jewish family in Berlin, whose affluence stemmed from his paternal grandfather. Between 1850 and 1890 his enterprises had expanded from a general store to a textile mill and then a tube-rolling mill for gas-pipe, which before this time had been hand-wrought in Germany [1]. His son, Oskar, continued the business and, in the course of trips to England, developed a fondness for its countryside and people which prompted him to build a summer residence near Wannsee Lake, in the traditional English country-house style with broad lawns, a rose-garden, a cricket ground and tennis courts, stables and orchards. Happy times boating on the lake and exploring the woods and countryside may have stimulated a fondness for outdoor life in Kurt and his two younger brothers.

The maternal grandparents grew up in Poland, assimilated to Polish society and sharing nationalist feelings against Russia, but retained roots in Jewish life. An ancestor, Chief Rabbi of Prague in the time of MariaTheresa, was credited with preventing the expulsion of Jews from that city. The family still had a portrait of this "Grand Rabby, professeur de Prague," an old man in a fur-trimmed black robe, his hand resting on a book of his writings [1]. The grandparents emigrated to Germany where their daughter, Charlotte, was born and where, at 18, she married Oskar Hahn. Later, after her busband's death, as Grandmother Anschulka, she joined her daughter's household in Berlin.

We have a glimpse of the Hahn family life from a memoir written by Sir Neville Butler while he was a guest in the house in 1915 [4]. An Oxford undergraduate, Butler had been trapped in Germany at the start of the war, and Kurt Hahn had intervened to obtain his release from internment camp on the condition that he stay in the Hahn residence. Eighteen years later, as private secretary to Ramsay MacDonald, Butler was able to persuade the prime minister to intervene effectively to bring about Hahn's release by the Nazis.

The 29-year-old Hahn was described as an impressive figure: "Strongly built, with a fine head protected by a drooping, broad-brimmed hat, walking with a slight stoop and a tread measured but capable of startling acceleration; a keen player of tennis and hockey, a sprinter and jumper (standing jump preferred) but keeping athletics well in its place." Kurt's father had died during his student days, and the household now consisted of his mother, 87-year-old grandmother, an amamuensis for Kurt and an attendant for the grandmother and, intermittently, two younger brothers who had joined the armed forces. Kurt was exempt from military service because of earlier cranial surgery for a complaint the nature of which is not clear to me. Anschulka, autocrat of the dinner table, was evidently a constant source of wise sayings, old stories, and Polish proverbs [1]. Kurt would sometimes fabricate some startling news when his grandmother was in a gloomy mood. To this end he once confided to her that [4] "he was engaged to be married. Frau Landau became all afire with interest and after a while demanded to see a photograph of the young lady. Kurt produced a portrait of Mrs. Winston Churchill and no exception was taken to this on the grounds of looks. But Frau Landau elicited further that the parents were not particularly nice but exceedingly wealthy. On these grounds she persuaded Kurt to break off the engagement." Forever after his grandmother believed he grieved for his lost sweetheart.

In fact Hahn did not ever marry, or apparently live intimately with a woman. Little has been reported about Hahn's early life, but I would guess that his relation to his mother played an important role. Charlotte Hahn had married at just 18, and Kurt was born a year later. She was an accomplished pianist and gathered many eminent scholars, politicians and artists in her home. She had a spellbinding influence on all her chil-

dren. Her relationship with Kurt was has been described as like that of an elder sister or a best friend. They understood one another without needing to speak.

Perhaps there are echoes of this in the loyalty and, sometimes, stronger emotional ties with the many women associated with him in Salem school and its various progeny, as teachers, staff and less formal supporters. Foremost among these relationships was unquestionably that with his brother's wife, and later widow, Lola Warburg-Hahn. She was also a sister of Eric Warburg, a German banker who played a vital role over many years as financial adviser to Salem. Eric had escaped Germany at the very last moment, reaching New York in September 1939. The moment the war was over Hahn wanted to return and help restore Salem, but the British would not give a travel permit as he was considered pro-German. But as an intelligence officer in the US Air Force Eric was able to bring him back to Germany and together they negotiated removal of the 600 French soldiers billeted at the school [5].

Something of the relationship between Hahn and Lola was eloquently recorded by David Sutcliffe at her Memorial Service in 1989 (5): "Lola became his sister-in-law, his sister, his platonic wife (if that is not too outrageous a term), later his mother.... Kurt became crucially dependent on her.... Kurt spent most of his life fund-raising. For his entire life he was kept by Rudo and Lola.... She said of him: 'I cannot help but feel that Kurt was not so naive about money; there was a shrewdness, and he certainly took with a smile advantage of Rudo and myself.'... What kind of a partnership was this between Kurt and Lola ? Well ... the task was to 'kindle' people; the measure of men was whether they 'burned for the cause.'... Was it a spiritual relationship? Perhaps, but one without illusions.... He was often a little frightened of her. Once, when she was due to visit him at the Hermansberg for three or four days, he told his secretary to hang all the pictures crooked: 'it will keep her busy for at least the first half day.' At a moment when he was greatly concerned about her health he wrote her: 'I need you. Please remember that' "

The letter sounds a note that is heard again in other relationships, as in the following anecdote by a director of studies at Gordonstoun school (4). The wife of a former colleague, who was in his late eighties, had written at Christmas that her husband "was dying, that he had made his peace with his Maker, and was ready to die." In the Spring he met Hahn, who asked if he had seen their colleague. "I said that he was dying and that I did not wish to intrude. 'Nonsense', Hahn replied, 'he is much better and you must see him.' So I went ... and there he was, walking about and in remarkably good health. When he was out of the room I asked Bee about it and she replied: 'Alec was dying as I told you. Then Hahn came to see him, and told him that he was needed and could not possibly die.'" The anecdote also illustrates an educational principle that Hahn often affirmed (6): "There are three ways of trying to win the young. There is persuasion, there is compulsion and there is attraction. You can preach at them, that is a hook without a worm; you can say 'You must volunteer,' that is of the devil; and you can tell them 'YOU ARE NEEDED!' That appeal hardly ever fails."

But to return to Lola: she was from the vast Warburg clan of bankers influential in several German cities as well as New York and London (Ron Chernow, *The Warburgs*). None of this clan was lost in the holocaust. Many of their children went to Hahn's schools at Salem and Gordonstoun. Throughout the thirties in Germany Lola was totally preoccupied with trying to succor Jews and aid their emigration. An ardent Zionist, she had a brief affair with Chaim Weizmann, and visited Palestine with him. I must apologize for having found no record of Hahn's reaction to the religious and political sympathies of the person closest to him throughout his adult life. The story of "Hahn as a Jew" must be left for someone else. It is obvious that by the time he founded Salem his enthusiasm for Christian moral teaching had gone far enough beyond "assimilation" that his later conversion to the Church of England should have caused little surprise.

But a few of his recorded remarks do surprise me. One is an oft-quoted and highly adulatory letter to Konrad Lorenz (Austrian 1972 Nobel laureate for discoveries in animal behavior). Lorenz's publications during the Nazi period had encouraged their racial policy (Richard Lerner, *Final Solutions*): "Protection of the race requires more stringent elimination of the ethically less valuable—We must charge our Best with the extermination of the population loaded with dregs." He did not recant these views after the war, and in his 1966 book *On Aggression* effectively absolved the Germans from any guilt for following Hitler, claiming they had been forced to do so by a universal human instinct.

I have also come across no mention of the holocaust by Hahn, except once in later years, when he seemed to conclude that it had been morally less heinous than the American use of the atomic bomb in Japan. I am familiar with the controversy over whether and how to use the bomb, and find Hahn's view very strange indeed. The leaders who prevailed in its use knew nothing of the long-term radiation effects, and could see it only as a supplement to the air force bombings that had already damaged nearly all other Japaneses cities, in a policy guided by a need to bomb something if only to justify the cost of the huge bomber force. No doubt there are those still living who could bring insight to these apparent aberrations, and to Hahn's feelings about his Jewish origins.

By common agreement two experiences played a decisive role in guiding Hahn's perspective in the founding of Salem school. The first was the impressions of English life gained from his four years at Oxford immediately before World War I, and the second was the war itself, and his exposure to German policies and public figures dominant in the last days of the empire of Wilhelm II.

Hahn went to Oxford in 1910 on the advice of a professor at Göttingen under whom he was studying Greek, who advised him that the German universities could not help if he was interested in the old in order to help the new. Between the ages of 24 and 28 he pursued his studies of philosophy and classics there. He read Greek throughout his life, and often quoted a maxim from Pindar: "Grow into what you are." What Hahn understood by this exhortation, which had puzzled nineteenth century Greek scholars and was probably not clarified when Nietzsche chose it as the subtitle of his autobiography, is indicated by the more explicit motto chosen later for Gordonstoun, the British school he founded after his escape from Germany: *Plus est en vous* (you have more in you than you think).

Plato's influence on Hahn is also often emphasized, as illustrated by the choice of the word "Guardian" for the appointed head of the student body, but the influence could be easily exaggerated: the pragmatist was impatient with anything calling itself a "philosophy" of education.

Hahn had resolved to be a schoolmaster long before his years at Oxford. Jocelin Winthrop-Young, who was my classmate in 1933 and whom I met again in 1991 when he was collecting the school archives at Salem, described how this came about in an eloquent memoir written on the 100th anniversary of the founding of Salem [7]:

"In 1902 Hahn went on a walking tour in the Dolomites with three old boys from Abbotsholme. Their account of this (English) school, which had been founded in 1889 by Cecil Reddie, filled him with enthusiasm. Herman Lietz had worked there for a year and written a book about his visit which they gave Hahn to read. One can imagine his excitement when he read the following:

'It appears to me tonight as though I had spent a day in a small Ideal State. How I wish that everything in the great world were arranged as it is in this small community! How healthy are the citizens, and how excellently is their work adapted to the age of each! How well they organize their little world! How courageously they fought for it in the football match! How keen they were in practicing for the match beforehand! What a fine thing it is for them that they are warriors, artists, laborers, craftsmen, government officials, teachers, judges and merchants, all in one! What splendid comradeship reigned in this state! To me that appeared to be the prevailing idea in it. How kindly the older boys helped the youngsters at their work! I felt in this little state as though I had joined a large family. A common love for worth, ability and thoroughness seemed to bind all its members together.'"

Jocelin continued: "In November 1904 Hahn writes to a friend: 'I have given up the idea of becoming an art historian and want to be a schoolmaster, not a Royal Prussian teacher but an educator and teacher under Lietz and later on my own.' Thus at the age of eighteen Hahn had decided on his career, though it was to take fourteen more years before he was able to start."

Later while at Oxford Hahn also came to admire England's more traditional boarding schools, as well as the less traditional Abbotsholme school, and resolved to found a school incorporating features of both in Germany, where country boarding schools were little known. Many years later he described the characteristics he had admired in the best of the English boarding school graduates [8]: "Confidence in effort, modesty in success, grace in defeat, fairness in anger, clear judgement even in the bitterness of wounded pride, readiness for service at all times." In the same radio talk he expressed some regret that these schools had been "isolated adolescent communities," but acknowledged that Salem had later also not entirely succeeded in his goal of service to the community.

Hahn made many friends and influential contacts during his years at Oxford and summers in Scotland, and thus Salem had from the beginning exchange programs for students and staff from English schools. From participation in Student Union debates he also acquired an admiration for the English parliamentary system of government, in which he saw aristocracy and democracy complementing each other. But among his friends he probably preferred the gentlemen of England to her commoners.

When the war began Hahn returned to Germany and, exempt from military service because of physical disability, was assigned in Berlin to analyze the English press for the foreign office. The quality of his reports brought him into contact with infuential leaders in the Kaiser's regime, and he acquired a political intuition and skill at influencing events from behind the scenes, a flair for reaching leaders through their subordinates. In 1917 he protested unrestricted submarine warfare, as an act that would guarantee Germany's defeat by bringing America into the war. He was deeply impressed to discover that many in power knew this and agreed with him but dared not speak out. The need to educate people who would act upon their convictions was, I believe, the primary force behind Hahn's prompt defiance of Hitler following the Potempa muder. As he repeated again and again [8]: "The worth of a faith does not consist in the clarity with which it is stated but in the steadfastness with which it is defended."

As a result of Hahn's memo on submarine warfare he lost his job, and was reassigned as an aide to the political advisor to General Ludendorf. There he could help achieve his goal throughout the war, a negotiated peace with England. An opportunity opened briefly at the end of 1917 through the revolution in Russia, and unofficial overtures from the Foreign Secretary Lord Lansdowne in the British press. Ludendorf was opposed to postponing his last fatal offensive of March 1918, but Hahn felt he could have been persuaded to wait for a political offensive first; once again the civilian authorities knew what should be done but failed to act. When Max von Baden was appointed Imperial Chancellor in October 1918, Hahn became his personal secretary. By now Ludendorf's offensive had failed and he had requested the armistice which, the historian Golo Mann believes, lost Germany the opportunity to negotiate at Versailles. Ludendorf later wrote a pamphlet in which he blamed Germany's defeat on "jesuits, freemasons and Jews." Perhaps this is the reason that the Bodensee Rundschau article mentioned earlier accused Hahn of being a freemason as well as an arch-Jew. In November 1918 revolution broke out in Germany, Max von Baden retired in favor of a Social Democrat leader, and withdrew to his castle at Salem near the Bodensee.

The castle and estate of the Markgraf of Baden (Markgraf is an ancient German title in the landed German aristocracy, which has no counterpart in the English peerage) offered a splendid site for the boarding school which Prince Max and Kurt Hahn now proceeded to establish. Adjoining the vast castle were the buildings of an ancient Cistercian monastery, which came to the Baden family when Napoleon undertook to consolidate some of the 300-odd independent principalities then composing what is now Germany. Thus the Margraves came into posession of a cathedral dating from 1296, which to this day serves as their private chapel, as well as the monastery rebuilt about 1700, with its Langbau structures well suited for use as student housing and classrooms. In December 1919 Prince Max established an endowment of 800,000 marks for a school "to be located in Salem, and to create an opportunity for higher education for the youth of the Salem valley, and beyond that to provide opportunities for education and instruction to other natives of Baden, particularly the sons of officers killed in action [5]."

The school opened on 21 April 1920 with 20 pupils, boys and girls, 8 of them boarders. It is memorable that a Salem hockey club had started

training even 6 months before the school started. Hahn had enjoyed field hockey at Oxford, and played on the Gordonstoun school team until he was 50. "The first match was on 26 October 1919. All the details of this event have survived including the first of his renowned hockey critiques stuck on the noticeboard after matches. Prince Max was in goal, and Fraulein Ewald much praised as center half " [7]. Later Hahn's critiques and encouragements at hockey games became legendary [4]: "Don't Jacksonise, Jackson, you are playing like a jellyfish on a holiday!" and "Run, run with the speed of ten antelopes."

In making Salem coeducational, Hahn relied heavily on Frl. Ewald (who was to become Headmistress of the branch I was enrolled at in 1933). She wrote later [1]: His "attitude to girls was peculiar to him. On the one hand he held them responsible for the tone of the school and even for callousness by other pupils of which they had been in complete ignorance. On the other hand he was capable of ignoring them completely." Later Gordonstoun school in Scotland was opened for boys only, partly because Frl. Ewald had not been able to follow him from Germany, but also because he did not want it labeled as a "progressive" school.

Hahn invoked Plato on the specific virtue of a boarding school in separating children from parents during the years of decisive development [9]. Its function, he claimed, should be to strengthen the influence of the healthy parental home, to supplement the influence of the well-meaning but inadequate home, and to compensate for the defective home [10].

A few words about the 19th century development of German schools will help to put Salem in perspective. In 1815 the Prussian 8-year elementary schools renamed Volksschulen became models for the other states and by 1830 illiiteracy was almost zero in Germany, in contrast to 40% in England in 1860, and 55% in France in 1870 (Gordon Craig, *Germany, 1866-1945*). German universities were the best in Europe, though given the reactionary government, most professors were conservative, antisemitic and enthusiasts for colonial expansion. The Volksschulen instilled discipline, order and obedience to authority, and until uniifcation in 1870 taught the three R's, religion and singing, after which history and science were added, though these subjects were devoted to fighting socialism. University access was through the Gymnasia, which drew their students from private schools, and a few at age 10 from Volksschulen. Working class students at university increased their proportion from 0.1 to 1 % during the last decade.

By 1930 about a dozen country boarding schools had appeared in Germany, as alternatives to the authoritarian state school system with its emphasis on docile compliance and humiliating drill.

In the first years Hahn also continued to serve as private secretary to Prince Max collaborating on his voluminous memoirs.The dual roles of teaching and being involved in public affairs were always seen as advantageous to the former as, by keeping the students directly in touch with current affairs, they diminished the character of "isolated adolescent community" that seemed an unfortunate aspect of the typical English boarding school. In 1929 Prince Max died and was succeeded by his 24-year-old son Berthold, who had been a student in the first year class and had held the position of "Guardian," the appointed head of the student body.

The school expanded rapidly in the first decade, opening three new branches in the nearby countryside (a fifth branch, Birklehof, drifted apart from Salem). All occupied relatively ancient and venerable buildings. Two junior schools were established: at Hohenfels, a former castle of the Knights of the Teutonic order, and Hermansberg, a former convent which was Hahn's personal property and where he maintained his apartment. A second senior school for 13- to 19-year-olds was established at Spetzgart (also an ancient church property but now dating mostly only from about 1800) on the outskirts of Überlingen on the shore of the Bodensee. This was the branch which I entered in May of 1933. With Frl. Ewald as director, Spetzgart was thought of as a test to see whether the "Salem method" could prosper without the physical presence of Hahn. Total enrollment in the four schools had grown from 20 to 426 at my arrival.

This rapid growth occured under remarkably adverse conditions. Hahn characterized the decade as a time when [11] "All of the sores of our history seemed to open up again. There was a class war of unheard-of bitterness, there were intense religious feuds, at the same time a triumphant progress of cynicism—among the right-minded no desire for a combined effort to defend what was once sacred to the nation. One felt inclined to quote Bismarck's cruel words: 'If two Germans agree they quarrel why they agree.'" Meantime the school's initial endowment had vanished through hyperinflation long before the exchange rate peaked in November 1923 at 2.5 billion marks per dollar. The worldwide depression that followed in 1930 was likewise not favorable to the expansion of an expensive boarding school.

Anecdotes illustrate the austerity of student life in the early days and even in my year there. Frl. Ewald remembered that the school had only one lamp when it opened, so that evening study was all done in one room, the baroque former Abbot's apartment. Golo Mann wrote that when he was at Salem in 1923 students brought silverware or other household posessions for tuition, and that he himself paid ten American dollars for one semester.

Map of the Salem schools: Salem, Spetzgart and Hohenfels are circled

Fees were graded according to the income of the parents. In his radio talk in 1934, describing the Salem system he hoped to introduce in his new Scottish school Hahn said [11]: "In their own interest and in the interest of the nation, children of the powerful and the secure ought to share the experiences of an enthralling school life with the sons and daughters of those who have to struggle for their existence. During the first years at Salem 30 per cent of our children came from homes where life was not only simple but hard. Secondly, we had a day school attached to Salem, the children, for the most part, coming from self-respecting peasant homes, bringing with them a definitely critical attitude that means daylight at times strong enough to dispel the two spectres inevitably haunting every successful boarding school, self-satisfaction and self-deception."

A key innovation at the Salem schools was the plan to divide authority equally between two directors (in turn responsible to the principal), a director of studies in charge of teaching in the usual sense, and a director of miscellaneous "activities". Sometimes the Headmaster also served in the latter capacity. The two directors were intended to have comparable power in the event of conflict, as illustrated by the reminiscence of a Gordonstoun teacher [12]: "I remember being somewhat surprised when Dr. Hahn offered me the post of Director of Studies at Gordonstoun in 1935, that he added: 'You must defend your department. If I want to send a boy for health reasons into the hills for three weeks just before his examination you must resist me.'" Many of the staff had responsibilities in both the academic and the activities programs, and recruiting people suitable for both was a challenge, especially in Germany. Even to this day Salem finds suitable candidates more easily in England and America.

Granted the successful recruitment of suitable teachers, the classroom program was relativelty conventional, directed towards the requirements for the Abitur, the government-awarded School Leaving Certificate based on a standardized examination that all students had to pass in their final year to be admitted to a University. At Salem Hahn himself taught English and History of the First World War. Golo Mann also remembers a Latin class, studying Caesar's Gallic War [13]: "If he wanted us to translate into Latin, he made up texts that dealt with life at the school and contained quotations from members of the class. For instance, he had me comment thus on an impending hockey game: 'I cannot take part in the game because while playing I can see only the one opponent to be killed.'"

One of Hahn's innovations was his progressive granting of student privileges and responsibities. New pupils were to wear their own clothes for a time after arrival, then would don the school uniform, signaling their membership in the community. The uniform could be taken away for such things as cheating or lying. After the uniform, the second step was the granting of the Training Plan, intended to encourage students, through trust, to exercise self-supervision. In this plan the students prepared a calendar where with a plus or minus they recorded daily compliance with various rules or duties. On demand, a student had to produce it and discuss it with his housemaster, but it was mainly the student's private concern. Here are the rules from a sample Training Plan: "One warm wash, no eating between meals, report illness, rope-climbing, account book, special duties." The Training Plan, much debated by other educators, grew out of Hahn's sense of the prevalence and danger of self-deception, and the importance of learning to recognize one's own weaknesses. If disciplinary offenses transgressed not only regulations but moral principles, the well-being of the school as well as the student's future were felt to be at stake, and Hahn did not rest until all the implications of such an offence had been understood by everyone, both students and teachers. What was meant by "all the implications" comes alive from Jocelin Winthrop-Young's [7)] memory of "Those long exhausting rows when he tried to get a total understanding of oneself by oneself.... To admit to a misdemeanour, to excuse oneself, to accept the punishment was all not enough. He wanted more, he wanted the full acknowledgement of one's own weaknesses; the conquest of self-deception." In the early days at least serious offenses, and the punishment inflicted, were posted on the bulletin board. Sometimes the whole school had to stand in silence for half an hour or more while Hahn was elucidating the facts and deciding how to deal with them.

After receiving the Training Plan a student was eligible to be a member of the Color Bearers, an upper body or Senate comprising about one-fourth of the students in my time. The Color Bearers, who wore a purple stripe on the school uniform, were elected by their own members as vacancies occured, on the basis of the individual's character and loyalty and service to the school, and were entrusted with maintaining law and order as well as unwritten laws and principles. A few of the staff were also members. The headmaster was chairman of the Color Bearers meetings, and the vice-chairman was the "Guardian" (head boy or girl) appointed by the headmaster. This prefect system was inspired by traditional English boarding schools, but "Hahn's brilliant trick was to transfer ministerial portfolio to the prefects—there were to be no pupils holding authority without specific jobs" [7]. Hahn described some of the Color Bearer's responsibilities at Salem in 1934 as: prefect of juniors, to safeguard the interests of younger students against masters and seniors; prefect of health, to look after convalescents and supervise remedial exercises of students with disabilities; prefect of outposts, to look after day students and visit them in their homes; prefects to be in charge of waste management, heating systems, buildings and grounds. On Sundays each color bearer was expected to go on a solitary walk lasting two hours.

In recent times the English schools modeled on Salem have tended to retain this elitist separateness of the Color Bearers, favoring effective administration but with the danger of becoming too distant from the other students. The advantage that each generation is encouraged to redefine the school principles by reflecting on what constitutes the qualification for holding the colors has not always been reflected by a rate of resignation consistent with honest self-criticism [7]. The German schools have abandoned the Color Bearers, and today all student officers are elected by the whole student body.

When students left Salem they received not only the final grades from the official Abitur examination, but in addition a "Final Report to Parents." The sample report I am looking at shows that individual grades were to be recorded for achievement in craft work, art and music, and physical exercises (under fighting spirit, endurance and reaction time) but beyond these also for: Public spirit; Manners; Sense of justice; Ability to state facts precisely; Ability to plan; Imagination; Ability to deal with the unexpected; Degree of mental concentration - where the task in question interests him/her, and where it does not; Conscientiousness—in everyday affairs, and in tasks with which he/she is specially entrusted; Ability to follow out what he/she believes to be the right course in the face of (separate grade for each hurdle)—discomforts, hardships, dangers, mockery, boredom, skepticism, impulses of the moment.

Clearly education for life was considered, at Salem, at least as important as education of the mind, so it is not surprising that even beyond the school years certain obligations were proposed to Salem alumni to be followed during their university years: each year a month of strenuous physical training with no cigarettes or drinking, three months work in a factory, and 6 weeks in a "sailing, flying or riding school [13]." In Golo Mann's memoir we learn that he did indeed spend the summer of 1928 working in a coal mine after his graduation but this alumni training program must have been one of the first casualties after 1932.

By his own account and those of his colleagues, Hahn had no "theory" of education, and considered originality to be as out of place in education as in medicine. He often quoted Prince Max's reply to an "over-enthusiastic" American visitor's question about what he was most proud of in the school [6]: "There is nothing original. That is what I am proud of. We have stolen from everywhere."

To convey Hahn's conception of the "Principles of Salem," I come now to a typewritten document from the school archives, cited in some bibliographies as having been composed by him in 1930. It reads as follows:

THE SEVEN LAWS OF SALEM

FIRST LAW:

Give the children opportunities for self-discovery.

Every girl and boy has a "grande passion," often hidden and unrealized to the end of life. The Educator cannot hope and may not try to find it out by psycho-analytical methods. It can and will be revealed by the child coming into close touch with a number of different activities. When a child has come "into his own," you will often hear a shout of joy, or be thrilled by some other manifestation of primitive happiness. But these activities must not be added as a superstructure to an exhausting program of lessons. They will have no chance of absorbing and bringing out the child unless they form a vital part of the day's work. The wholesome passion once discovered grows to be "the guardian angel" of the years of adolescence, while the undiscovered and unprotected boy rarely maintains his vitality unbroken and undiluted from 11 to 15. We do not hesitate to say: often the spiritual difference in age between a boy of 15 and a boy of 11 is greater than that of a man of 50 and a boy of 15.

SECOND LAW:

Make the children meet with triumph and defeat.

Let them learn to "treat these two imposters just the same." It is possible to wait on a child's inclinations and gifts and to arrange carefully for an unbroken series of successes. You may make him happy that way—I doubt it—but you certainly disqualify him for the battle of life. Salem believes you ought to discover the child's weakness as well as his strength. Allow him to engage in enterprises in which he is likely to fail, and do not hush up his failure. Teach him to overcome defeat. "To him that overcometh will I give to eat of the tree of life." Rev. 2-7.

THIRD LAW:

Give the children the opportunity of self-effacement in the common cause.

Even the youngsters ought to undertake tasks which are of definite importance for the community. Tell them from the start:"You want a crew, not passengers on the thrilling voyage to the new country school." Let the responsible boys and girls shoulder duties big enough, when negligently performed, to wreck a state.

FOURTH LAW:

Provide periods of silence.

Following the great precedent of the Quakers. Unless the present day generation aquires early habits of quiet and reflection, it will be speedily and prematurely used up by the nerve exhausting and distracting civilization of today.

FIFTH LAW:

Train the imagination.

You must call it into action, otherwise it becomes atrophied like a muscle not in use. The power to resist the pressing stimulus of the hour and the moment can not be aquired in later life; it often depends on the ability to visualize what you plan and hope and fear for the future. Self indulgence is in many cases due to lack of vision: *"Wer das ferne nicht bedenkt, dem ist betrübnis nahe."*

SIXTH LAW:

Make games important but not predominant.

Athletics do not suffer by being put in their proper place. In fact you restore the dignity of the usurper by dethroning him.

SEVENTH LAW:

Free the sons of the wealthy and powerful from the enervating sense of priviledge.

Decadence is not always an inexorable decree of nature, more often it is a wilfull waste of a splendid heritage. The "poor" rich girls and boys wholly thrown into each other's company are not given a chance of growing into men and women who can overcome. Let them share their experiences of an enthralling school life with sons and daughters of those who have to struggle for their existence. No school can build up a tradition of self-discipline and vigorous but joyous endeavour,

> unless at least 30% of the children come from homes where life is not only simple but even hard.

Hahn was unlikely to forget for a moment that the realization of "principles" must be circumscribed by the limitations of real students and teachers. To anyone agitated by these limitations he offered a favorite adage: "human nature is very prevalent."

Sixty years ago Hahn could characterize the goal of the school as "character training." Apparently even then some senior students felt opressed by the sense that they were expected to become "trained for leadership." In keeping with the evolving *zeitgeist* Hahn later changed the words, if not the concept, to "training for service." I remember service work as farm chores for tenants on the Markgraf's estates, or domestic chores for the girls. Later "service" evolved into things more congenial to the ear today, ministering to the poor, elderly and sick. The story of the Good Samaritan was his favorite homily; later as he became involved in projects that led to the Outward Bound movement he became deeply impressed by rescue work. Its transforming effect on the rescuer captured his imagination, and he came to think it could yield more dramatic changes in the young than community service.

Hahn also provided opportunities to pursue hobbies and students and staff could initiate "guilds," which dealt with a school magazine or library, or projects in natural science, painting, music or drama. Hahn's early involvement in amateur theatricals stimulated a serious investment in student musical and dramatic performance.To me these performances seemed to have some flavor of the 18th century court of the Duchy of Weimar in Goethe's time. In the early days after the war the Rütli scene from *William Tell*, and Yeats' drama *Cathleen ni Houlihan* about Irish independence, were popular. Later thousands came to see an annual nativity play at Christmas, brought back to the Bodensee from where the Protestant refugees had originally carried it to Hungary in the 16th century, the audience from the Salem valley still able to understand the old dialect. Similar audiences came every summer for a Greek tragedy or Shakespeare play performed outdoors in front of the castle.

Craftwork could either stimulate a student's liflelong "grand passion", or alternatively implant confidence to overcome deficiency of skill. Originally Prince Max had spoken of students going to workshops of the artisans of the Salem valley: the bookbinder, builder, blacksmith, cabinet maker and wood carver, where he said they would learn a "horror of half-finished work" [11]. In my time, thirteen years later, the blacksmith and cabinet maker came to shops at the school.

At Salem organized games were not to be allowed to begin before age thirteen. In 1934 Hahn said [11]: "We find the boy and girl of six hardly ever bored by empty hours. We find them forever dreaming, planning, building, discovering, asking, singing and making-believe. Then suddenly all that stops together. The child home for the holidays does not know what to do with himself. Why? Organized games have begun too early. They do not neccessarily damage the dreamer who takes refuge from the games in a safe and secret corner of his own. They damage the boy athlete who is thrilled by his football experiences and lured away from his own creative passions till one day they are no longer capable of revival. (Later) we found it neccessary to dethrone games even in the senior schools. We rationed them. They are compulsory on two days a week. On other week days, and as a rule also on Sunday, they are not allowed. We were prepared for a lessened efficiency in games but the result was the opposite. Our games, by being rarer, have become more dignified and festal."

In place of competitive games, the school placed great stress on the athletic training of those who were not naturally keen nor particularly gifted in sports. There was a long run every morning before breakfast, regardless of weather. Continuing in the radio talk of 1934 [11]: "We are able to teach practically all the boys to sprint, to jump and to throw. We make them do it all the year around four times a week during the 'break' in the morning and we find that with 90 per cent it is possible to build up a resisting and resilient power. The high jump is especially fitted to develop power of decision. The boy of refined intellect often shrinks from this test at the beginning and inasmuch as he overcomes his aversion to gathering up his strength in face of an obstacle the life of action begins to attract him. We have cured a stammerer by the high jump. In 1928, 80 per cent of the boys who left us could jump over 5 feet." Each participant in these daily training exercises competed only against his or her own previous record. Hahn is said to have often attended, encouraging especially the less succesful to greater efforts.

Later chapters taken from the diary I kept at Salem in 1933-34 will make it plain that "Adventures" were the part of he school program that I found by far the most intriguing. Expeditions, ad hoc improvisations by staff and students, imaginative responses to unforseen happenings—these defy generalization. In later years, as the Outward Bound movement began to emerge in England, Hahn became the world leader in the use of adventure to educate the young.

I return now to Hahn's famous 1932 circular letter to Salem alumni, quoted at the beginning, in which in response to Hitler's glorification of the Potempa murderers he asked all alumni to terminate their allegiance either to Hitler or to the school. What were some of the reactions of his supporters, at the time and later? What might have been predominant in the thoughts and beliefs that led him to take this step?

A British colleague wrote that [1]: "We in this country should realize the courage that lay behind it. It was a very solitary action," and Sir Robert Birley continued with an interesting speculation: "Salem was a school of considerable renown, but its Association had no standing comparable with that of certain societies connected with the German universities, the famous Altherrenverbände. If one of these societies of past university students had taken such a step, the effect in Germany would have been profound. As far as I know, such action was never even contemplated." From one point of view, Hahn's letter to Salem alumni may have been seen as a simple act of solitary heroism. There is said to be a British tendency to see the rest of the world as more like England than it is. German colleagues might even have added that, as a result of his Oxford years, Hahn himself saw Germany as more English than it was, when he wrote, as if to the *Times*, a dignified reply to the article in the Bodense Rundschau that had described him as "a freemason and arch-Jew (who) in his hatred of Germany ... will pursue Hitler like a plague." The Rundschau did not print his reply. Golo Mann later expressed a German view of such correspondence [1]: "What ... saddens us is that Hahn still fought against such infamies, that he seriously disputed the lies put out against him ... that he corresponded and exchanged pamphlets with 'wolves, swine and dirty dogs'—to quote a poet he dislikes."

A German colleague, writing almost 50 years later [14] remembered the letter to the alumni quite differently, as a reckless throwing of the gauntlet to Hitler. Wilhelm Kuchenmüller, a Salem teacher about whom more will be said later, had been a Nazi party member from the early days, and was expelled in 1933 because of his defense of Hahn, at the first moment when membership might have been to his advantage. He thought Hahn could have chosen a more prudent and effective course, and recollected his feelings on January 30th 1933 when Hitler was appointed chancellor: "For Salem (it) was not a day of celebration. Salem was Hahn and Hahn was a Jew. He himself was one of the utopians who believed he could stay at his post. In that belief he had mustered everything a moment before midnight in order to hinder Hitler's victory. Dangerously overestimating his possibilities, he had stepped out from his usual position behind the scenes to throw the gauntlet to Hitler."

Hahn released the alumni from his injunction to choose between Hitler and Salem in letters written in June 1933 to parents and friends [9]: "Salemers today are free to join the SA or the SS. Why today and not in

August 1932? Because today you can summon Hitler to oppose indefensible principles." His challenge to the Nazis was not muffled. Two weeks after Hitler came to power he said, in a public lecture on Italian Fascism [1)], that beside "sacred egoism" there was also "sacred lying, sacred killing, sacred perjury, sacred breaking of promises." But Hahn looked for the best in everyone, and people often tried to live up to his assesment. The worst he would say of an opponent was "I do not include him in my prayers." He wanted to believe that in the end a better Hitler would metamorphose from the bad Hitler. Many at this time also believed Hitler might soon be voted out again, or be pushed aside by somone else from within the Party. A party member from early days, Kuchenmüller had still hoped that a Freiherr vom Stein or a Bismarck would appear to replace Hitler [14]. Many Party faithful of similar views were to be shot in the purge of 1934.

What may have been going on in Hahn's mind at this time? The day after the 1930 election that gave the Nazis 18 per cent of the votes, he had written in a widely circulated letter [15]: "Today we confront a fascist upsurgence. What is the significance of 107 Nazi deputies? An unprecedented growth in the self-confidence of those dedicated to revolution by force. My uneasiness would be milder if I could say these enemies of the State are all idiots or scoundrels (but) the Nazi youth encompasses some of the best human potential. What is the real source of the powerful attraction of the Nazis? Apart from the economic privation it is disgust over the corruption of the German Parliamentary system. This system can no longer be retained."

To understand Hahn's position at this time one must briefly survey the last years of the Weimar Republic. Hahn was supporting a program that had been put into effect in 1930 by elements of the "old elite," drawn from the civil service, armed forces, employers and large landowners—the ruling classes under Bismarck and Wilhelm II—which undertook to reestablish under Chancellor Bruening an authoritarian regime which would govern without the Reichstag and combat the domestic welfare policies of the Social Democrats. Power was to be exercised by the elected president, Hindenburg, and a cabinet subject to his approval who could rule by emergency decree. Should a decree be over-ruled by a Reichstag majority, as the Weimar constitution permitted, the parliament could be dissolved. This provision for an "ersatz Kaiser" (article 48) was one of several defects in the Weimar constitution, which included also the ease with which issues could be referred to referenda or plebiscites, and the proportional representation which resulted in constantly shifting ad hoc coalitions of the many parties represented in the parliament.

But by 1932 the "old elite" had long since ceased to command any popular following, without which their reactionary program might eventually have satisfied the radical left's hope for a violent revolution. Meantime Hitler's share of the popular vote had further mushroomed from 18 to 35 percent. Supporters of the conservative "Presidential regime" calculated now to capture Hitler's popular following without yielding power, and accordingly when Hitler became chancellor in January 1933, only two out of six important cabinet positions were allotted to the Nazi party. He was to have been "framed-in" by the majority of reliable right-wing leaders.

His formative years passed in imperial Britain and Germany, Hahn was a monarchist at heart, who tended to reject the Weimar Republic and to condescend to its founding Social Democrats. Golo Mann believes that Hahn deceived himself. He seemed oblivious of the millions of Germans who voted socialist to the end, and "in his later years spoke of his organized efforts—indeed, of a conspiracy—to prevent Hitler from seizing power. But the aim of the 'conspiracy' he had in mind was too near to Hitler's to achieve its object. It was not to profit the 'laughing Left'—as if that were the danger in the autumn of 1932!—but the 'decent folk' among Hitler's supporters whom one hoped to entice away from him and rally to the Right's slogan of 'Presidential Government. Yet it was this very Right that made Hitler's seizure of power possible four months later [1]."

It may be that uneasy memories of his reactions to the Nazis had indeed nourished some self-deception. Perhaps these differing interpretations are best left to speak for themselves. I will give the last word to Meissner [16], who was to continue Salem's defiance of the Nazis for two more years, before he barely made his escape to join Hahn in Scotland: "Many friends of Salem, reasonable people, not born cowards, strongly disapproved of the circular letter [asking alumni to sever connections either with the school or the Nazi Party]. If Hitler comes to power, so they argued with the Headmaster, there will be revenge. You endanger yourself and the school and it is of no use to anybody. The cautious advisers were right in all they said about the probable results of the action. But the conclusions they drew were wrong. It is not right and proper to make success the supreme test of one's actions, and to refrain consequently from anything that might lead to failure. This frame of mind brings about defeat after defeat in public affairs. One fact is certain: the Nazis would not have been able to establish their regime had it not been for this widespread 'world-wise' timidity, which could be found everywhere: in the army, at the universities, among the civil servants, in industry."

Hahn had been released from prison on March 16, 1933, a week after his arrest, but exiled from Baden. In the ensuing months the issue became no longer that of the survival of Hahn but that of the survival of Salem. During these months a Nazi Kommissar had been installed and had suspended a number of the senior staff. The ensuing chaos will be described in later chapters, as I recorded it at the time in my diary, and as I learned more of it sixty years later from the school archives. The Markgraf Berthold, now 28 years old and married to a sister of the future Prince Phillip of England, had assumed responsibility for the school. The fact that some staff were maintaining telephone contact with Hahn in Berlin infuriated the Nazi authorities. In June 1933 the Markgraf wrote [7] to an English supporter, Geoffrey Young: "I think it is time for your friend Kurt to understand that his waiting will not help. It has become absolutely neccessary to convince him that he must leave his home country for a while." Hahn's reluctant departure for England, in the service of saving Salem more than of saving himself, did not suffice to end the conflict between the school and the Nazi regime. The second part of this book will detail how this conflict continued, through Salem's defiance and strategic accomodations, for twelve more years until the Allied defeat of Germany.

But we turn first to Hahn's career in England, where he now conceived and created a whole series of educational ventures based on the principles that he had evolved in Germany. Ventures that were to spread around the world and affect millions of young people.

CHAPTER 2

Hahn in Great Britain: Gordonstoun and Outward Bound

Within a year of his arrival in England, Hahn established a boarding school in the remote countryside of northeast Scotland. From this base he was to create out of the catastrophe of exile a series of educational projects that would spread around the world. Even when he retired to the Hermannsberg in Germany, after twenty years as Headmaster of Gordonstoun, he continued on into his eighties to maintain a sort of world headquarters at Brown's Hotel in London.

Now, it seems ironic that only fourteen years after founding a German school modeled on English schools, Hahn was urged to found an English school modeled on the principles of Salem! The prospects were much less promising. Germany had but a handful of country boarding schools, of recent origin, while in England there were well over a hundred such schools: some claiming five centuries of history and tradition (an important distinction later during the student unrest of the 1960s); some endangered by the continuing economic depression.

Besides the problem of soliciting financing from scratch, Hahn had lost all his personal assets. How this came about is suggested by the fate at this time of a prominent Jewish publisher, who was required to sell his $15 million firm to an Aryan buyer. Under the policy of Aryanization Jews were required to sell their assets to racially pure buyers for little or nothing. The best offer was $1.5 million, of which the publisher wound up with $25,000. But on trying to depart for England he was told he could not get a passport until he made "another sacrifice," a donation of $25,000 to the Berlin police. Fortunately for Hahn his sister-in-law Lola was lucky; despite an unfriendly aryanization she and her husband were able to live comfortably in England after they escaped in 1938 with 50% of their assets in the blast furnace he had inherited. The great Warburg Bank in Hamburg, valued at 12 million DM, fared less well in a "friendly" aryanization when their long-time-trusted Aryan associate

Brinckmann aquired it for 150,000. In the rubble of 1945 Brinckmann's offer to return the bank to Lola's brother Eric was declined. A few years later after the economic miracle Eric changed his mind, but Brinckmann now not unreasonably refused. Eric, the only Warburg to resettle in Germany and sometimes criticized for his cultivation of aristocratic circles there, was evidently also not one of the more talented of the banking clan—it was not until 1989 that his endless negotiations to recover the bank succceeded.

Temptation to despair yielded when Hahn discovered the possibility of occupying the buildings of an ancient, but empty and nearly derelict, estate near the spectacular sea cliffs along the Firth of Moray, and not far from the Cairngorm mountains. After securing a lease in March 1934 he agreed to open a school there as a temporary demonstration of Salem principles, and assembled a distinguished but hardly progressive board of governors that included the Archbishop of York, the Headmaster of Eton, a future Governor-General of Canada and the influential Oxford historian George Trevelyan.

"I have a dwarfish school at present, numbering five boys," Hahn wrote the parents of the fifteen-year-old Adam Arnold-Brown [17], who had been attending Abbotsholme. A description of this alternative English school had inspired Hahn thirty years earlier to become a teacher, but it had since suffered many vicissitudes. Visiting Gordonstoun in April, the boy found that Hahn seemed interested in him, included him in the conversation instead of talking only to his parents, and took him on a tour of secret passages, a dungeon, and an ancient circular stables built without corners for the devil to hide in. The choice was easy!

The school opened with a dozen German refugees and a similar number of boys who had failed to thrive at other English boarding schools. "No German spoken" was added to the self-graded Training Plan of the former. Two of the transfers from Salem had been schoolmates and friends of mine while I was there, and much will be heard of them later in my diary excerpts. They were Jocelin Winthrop-Young, who was to maintain a lifelong asociation with Hahn's schools and who introduced me to the Salem archives sixty years later, and Prince Philip of Greece, who was to become the spouse of the British monarch.

Hahn remarked that the school needed this brotherhood of nations and religions, but would have also to come to embody a brotherhood of classes, which was much more difficult to achieve. With its limited facilities Gordonstoun could not initially expect to have the pick of the country's pupils as Salem had had. Later it was recognized that the school often succeeded with boys with physical, intellectual or character handicaps, and it continued to make a place for them after it was no longer compelled to do so.

An American described Hahn as a man who had no small talk, ever. In the first months he seemed forlorn without someone to argue with in the German fashion. Meissner had held on at Salem for a year and a half after Hahn's departure, struggling to keep some control of the school. Openly defiant of the Nazis, he undoubtedly would have paid with his life had he not managed a secret crossing of the Swiss border. His arrival at Gordsonstoun gave a boost to Hahn's spirits. When Hahn would say later that he wanted it written on his tombstone: "He worked with Meissner for twenty years" (he had many proposals for his tombstone), he was recalling the arguments with a hint of complacency as well as exasperation.

Hahn is remembered quite differently in England than in Germany. From the German side one sees lengthy treatises on the influence of Plato, Rousseau, Goethe, Fichte, Pestalozzi, and William James, but little or nothing about the qualities of the man. For a portrait one must turn to anecdotes of English associates and students. Jocelin describes how Hahn appeared to the first Gordonstoun students [7]: "A big man with a slight stoop to his round head, which had little hair. The eyes were surprisingly bright blue. The hands were large and powrful and were folded over one another. The suit, worn loosely, was clearly tailor-made. The shoes had thick crepe soles which squeaked as he moved fast along the passages and warned us of his approach." Later, "He will remain a man who reads newspapers and not books. His library will contain the books he studied but will alter little. He has become an existentialist thinker dealing with the problems of the time."

Hahn was able to make Gordonstoun feel a part of the surrounding community, something not achieved at Salem. The Guardian's oath became: "I promise to serve Hopeman village and this district, through them my King and country, and Christ through all." Meissner said later that it had been founded as an English school; it was not just a repetition of Salem nor could it be. The self-selection of Colorbearers on the basis of character was, however, a novelty in England, where colors had been awarded solely for athletic achievement, as they are today in American High Schools. And so of course was Hahn's whole approach of dethroning games and emphasizing field and track training for the less gifted. Hahn may have felt refreshed by the difference between a German Gymnasium, enrolling only students aspiring, through the final state administered Abitur examination, to University admission, and an English private secondary school which could accomodate others who lacked academic aspiration or qualification. An American teaching at

Gordonstoun in 1951 [18], just before Hahn's retirement, found that "there were sons of bricklayers in the school who had aspirations different from their fathers', and there were others who intended also to be bricklayers. Both were equally honored."

Hahn became a British citizen in 1938, and a convert to the Church of England in 1945. But to the English colleagues who knew him best his way of thinking, his English style, his view of history, even his appearance remained distinctly German. According to English sensibilities, he sometimes expressed moral principles almost too earnestly. But the innovation initially most startling to English teachers was the separation of responsibilities for classroom and "other activities." To an English teacher who joined Hahn when he first came from Salem [12] "there seemed something quite bizarre about dividing the staff into 'teachers' on the one hand and 'character trainers' on the other. It seemed an insult to any schoolmaster to think he could teach without influencing character." Teachers in Germany had not had the background or inclination to take an active role in "other activities." A German critic is quoted [9] as contrasting them with the typical English teacher who "does not show an unseemly interest in his 'subject,' and who leads an all-around life in accord with the goals of his teaching." In the event the rigid segregation of character trainers from teachers was not long maintained in the new school.

Hahn reflected in 1950 that craftwork and hobby projects had done better at Salem [8], but the adventure and service parts of the "other activities" program had flourished in England, particularly through the opportunities for seamanship provided by the rough waters off the coast. Most mornings and afternoons in all seasons small boats were soon being launched from the fishing village of Hopeman two miles away, in seas much more challenging than the Bodensee. Enthusiastic now about the tranforming potentiality of rescue services, Hahn proposed in 1935 that the school start a Coast guard watch station. Suspicious at first, the boys were persuaded when two Coast guard officers came to tell them such a station was badly needed, and offered to provide pistols, rockets and breeches buoys if they would build a lookout hut. The watchers won the admiration of the Coastguard Service and though they were called out only three or four times a term, the lookout was henceforth manned in four hour shifts night and day. Teams became expert at cliff-ladder evacuation, and practiced running a breeches buoy on lines rocket-launched to offshore rocky islands

The first venture to encourage the principles of Salem in a larger community of youth beyond the limits of the boarding school came in

1936. A county award, the Moray badge was created to be awarded to boys in surrounding communities for performance in physical fitness (again emphasizing improvement among the less gifted), and for expeditionary and life-saving excercises. Gordonstoun's athletic facilities and student coaches were made available in the summer to pupils from other schools or boys already at work. It is often forgotten that this very least elitist, non-residential alternative to boarding schools, which today claims many millions of alumni all around the world, was conceived and initiated even before the short residential schools of Outward Bound. Hahn was to cherish and promote this program for the next seventeen years, before he finally succeeded in bringing it to life nation-wide as the Duke of Edinburgh Award Scheme.

Gordonstoun was in a militarily sensitive area, and on the outbreak of war, when enrollment had reached 135, the school was forced to evacuate by primarily local anti-German sentiment and suspicion of subversive activity. In 1940 five teachers and a number of boys were interned as enemy aliens. The school found a wartime sanctuary at Plas Dinam, the Welsh estate of a liberal internationally-minded parent. It was starting all over again: enrollment diminished by fifty, buildings widely scattered, new teachers to be found, financial jeapordy. The estate was far from the sea. Cutters were brought down by railroad from Scotland and dragged up a mountain side to a small lake, but eventually found a port at Aberdovey on Cardigan Bay, to which boys travelled thirty miles on week-ends for sailing. Under a skipper from the Blue Funnel Shipping Line boys sailed the Schooner flagship down from Scotland, out of touch for four days when it fell in with a convoy under blackout. It was this achievement which inspired Hahn and the owner of the shipping line to found the first Outward Bound School, the Aberdovey Sea School, in August 1941.

During the First War Hahn had worked behind the scenes with German leaders to promote a negotiated peace with England. Now he did not oppose the demand for unconditional surrender. In May 1945 he wrote in a diary [1]: "Without unconditional surrender there was no security for Britain, no liberation for Europe, no forgiveness for the German people ... my colleagues have prayed for the collapse of the Nazis for six years; I for twelve." At the same time he had hoped the Allies would be persuaded to cooperate with the leaders of the German resistance, and he had sought and nearly achieved a meeting with Churchill to this end. But during World War II, as in 1930, the resistance he had in mind was of the old elite—the military, civil service, large landowners and industrialists—who had enabled Hitler to seize power, though they did not share his racial obsession.

German members of the community had been released from internment in time to play a part in the British forces, and by the end of the war the school was more securely recognized and widely known, and substantially larger. Hahn insisted on returning to Scotland immediately, although there had been fire damage during army occupation, and the school had to be partly housed in Quonset huts while staff and students worked at restoration during summers. The school occupied scattered temporary quarters for fifteen years after the war, as enrollment grew to 400. The sailing program flourished as the school helped found an independent Outward Bound sea school next door, and boys from local fishing communities were enrolled in the student body through a new two- year vocational curriculum for merchant marine officers. After the success of the coastguard watch and shipwreck rescue activity in 1935, Hahn encouraged what he felt was the transforming effect of rescue services. A student fire-fighting brigade had already started in wartime Wales, when a senior boy painted his own ancient car red and equipped it with bell and small ladder. A mountain rescue service, which later became a ski patrol in the Cairngorm mountains, was started by Mr. Chew, and Beach Rescue was introduced later by a teacher from Australia.

An American impression of Hahn shortly before his retirement comes from the account [18] of a young teacher delegated, through the interest of the wives of the Ambassador to Great Britain and the High Commisioner of Germany in the new German Outward Bound Schools, to visit and report on Gordonstoun. Josh Miner was discouraged when, on his return he tried to introduce Salem principles at Andover Academy; a morning break for field and track exercise oriented to the less gifted gained reluctant acceptance when it turned out to improve classroom performance, but such innovation never caught on elsewhere. "Trespass continually," Hahn advised, when the disciple later explained he had been chary of trespassing in the province of classroom teachers. And in compliance a decade later, Miner was preeminently responsible for the explosive growth of the Outward Bound Movement in America.

Miner's mission to Gordonstoun began when he was met at the nearest train station by Hahn's driver, in a London taxicab. He explained that Hahn wanted them to get out of the car at various points on the way to the school to experience the vistas in the evening light. A student in the uniform of sky-blue shorts, shirt and sweater, who was the "Helper of Guests," met him when he finally arrived at 9:30, and led him "up a wide, highly-polished staircase. Creaking stairs, antiquity, and the pungent smell of floor wax. I found my host a bit daunting in the moment of meeting. I would learn not to be disconcerted by that trait of silent greeting that let the smile express it all - an expression that could go instantly from stern to amused and back. A big man. Great shoulders somewhat stooped. Large features and ears, the complexion startlingly soft and pink. Abetted by the three elderly ladies who were dining with him, he simultaneously plied me with questions about my family and bade me eat. I had scarcely slept in thirty-six hours, and on the forays from the car to view the evening light my feet had got wet." Presently Hahn asked him to step out in the hall, where he learned that the "Helper for Guests" had bicycled four miles to the guest house to fetch a pair of dry socks.

The next afternoon, touring the school with Humphrey, the "Helper," for a student eye view, he was told about the Training Plan, on which each student daily checked his own infractions. The penalty for lateness was to get up early for an extra long run, and Miner asked him why he didn't just skip doing his "lates," as he called them. "Come on, Humphrey," I said, "I would." Humphrey smiled. "I used to," he said, "but I got tired of lying to myself."

When Miner returned to Gordonstoun in 1951 to teach physics and math for a year, he was put in charge of the morning classroom break, where each boy competed against himself for an hour in field and track exercises. Every boy had to do every event; it was as important to overcome a weakness as to develop a strength. The frail youngster who broke ten feet in the long jump for the first time got as big a cheer as the star beating his previous mark of twenty. Miner was fascinated; the physical duffer had learned he could do better than he had dared dream, and began to shed "the misery of unimportance" (in Hahn's phrase) as new-found confidence carried over into peer relationships and classroom performance. Sometimes Hahn joined Miner at the morning break. Once, when a boy shied off after starting his high jump run, Hahn remarked: "The high jumpers love to dwell in the valley of indecision." And after a moment: "But they must commit themselves."

After a few months Miner became a housemaster and was promoted to replace Mr. Chew as Director of Activities. He observed how each night an older boy would come to a new student and check on his Training Plan. When the supervisor felt the newcomer could be responsible for grading himself, he reported that to the Helper of the House, who then persuaded Miner, who in turn would propose the promotion to Hahn. At that point Hahn would give Miner a thorough grilling; it was he, not the new boy, who was on trial.

Hahn, then sixty-five, was to serve several more years before his retirement from Gordonstoun. Besides running the school, he was making frequent trips to raise money for it and other projects, and shuttling across the channel to promote the Outward Bound schools in Germany.

But he found time to reconnoiter the school. "A headmaster's job," he said, "is to walk around." Sometimes at night several staff would be roused from slumber to come to Hahn's study. A boy was in trouble, he had spent a long evening talking with the boy and the student leaders who knew him best. Finally Hahn would ask Miner the dreaded question: "Josh! When did you first notice this boy was in difficulty and what did you do about it?" - dreaded because one had sensed and done nothing. It was not the boy but the adult community that was on trial.

As I end this acconut of Gordonstoun at the point of Hahn's retirement in 1953, it is time to look briefly at some criticisms that have been voiced over the years. Systematic objections to every aspect of Hahn's program have been published in Germany; I will touch on only a few points as, if I'm not mistaken, von Hentig [19] mostly accepts that the schools were what Hahn said they were. The reader, who by now shares this knowledge, can judge them for him or herself with the same credentials as the German critic. Amid all the publicity about adventure and rescue service, outsiders could forget that classroom work indeed existed at the schools, though the students were encouraged to think, rather than merely accumulate information. Still, intellectuals (whether children or adults) really did provide difficulties for Hahn, a distaste he rationalized by saying they lacked humility. [He himself wrote little, and probably would not have approved the writing of this book.] Looking back on a stint at Salem in the sixties, an alumnus said [9] "What did it offer the bookworm? I told my parents they would either have to take me out or I would provoke an expulsion."

Admission to Gordonstoun was based on interview only, contrasting with the competitive entry examinations of many private schools and Miner, in fact, found that he was teaching remedial arithmetic in 1952 to boys who would not have been academically qualified for most British or American private schools. Hahn believed admission based exclusively on mental ability was as immoral as admission based on the income of the students' parents.

"Confidence in effort, modesty in success, grace in defeat, fairness in anger, clear judgement even in the bitterness of wounded pride, readiness for service at all times." Such were the qualities Hahn attributed to graduates of English boarding schools, and wished to nourish when he opened Salem in 1920. A different aspect of these schools that has, however, consistently been cited by alumni, or at least by those that later take up writing, prompts one to hope that during the forty years since Hahn's departure Gordonstoun may have continued to oppose the bullying by older boys and erotic abuses so often described.

But here is a 1977 view from a Salem senior [9] after an exchange year at Gordonstoun two decades after Hahn's departure: "Living conditions are spartan. Students sleep in dormitory rooms with ten or more beds. There is no heating and no furniture besides the beds; any sign of individuality is forbidden. School uniform is obligatory, even off the school grounds. The catalogue of punishments is voluminous and the multitude of prohibitions in proportion. Instead of fellowship and fairness there is a pecking order in which the physically weaker must demonstrate their submissiveness."

A relative of Princess Diana has described Gordonstoun (*Newsweek*, 21 Dec. 1992) as "a very tough school with German tendencies. Prince Charles was bullied by the other boys. They continually held him upside down over the lavatory while they pulled the chain. He appealed to the headmaster, who said he saw no reason why he should interfere." Of course, popular perceptions may be inaccurate, and so may be *Newsweek's* accounts of them. But the headmaster at this time, Mr. Chew, is described by the Prince's biographer (Joanathan Dimbleby, *The Prince of Wales*) as "remote and austere ... gauche in his dealings with staff and pupils." Sadly different from my memories of Mr. Chew at Salem in 1933. (Yet it is true that when I once proposed visiting Gordonstoun during his tenure, his only reply was that "he could not remember me at all"—though he had been my Mentor in 1933, the teacher specifically responsible for my well being.)

How Hahn might have reacted under similar circumstances can be guessed from an incident in 1952, described again by Miner. A boy's behaviour had become so antisocial that the school could not keep him. After much effort, Hahn had found another school willing to take him, as he usually did when he had to expell a pupil. In a fury of spite on the day he was to leave, the boy made a shambles of his dormitory. When his housemates discovered the havoc, a group grabbed his arm and leg and started for the pond that underlay the school's rope climbing course. The Guardian was at some distance talking with companions when he saw what was happening. He watched as he continued talking. When he finally raced to break up the kangaroo court, he was too late. The boy had got his dunking. If a punishable offence took place in the Guardian's presence, only he was punished, and Miner was astonished at the severity of Hahn's penalty. He not only relieved the Guardian of his post, he took away his Training Plan. The senior was not punished for his failure to prevent the dunking; his offence, said the bulletin board notice, was that he had hesitated before trying to prevent it.

Prince Charles was not happy at Gordonstoun, but before putting all the blame on changes in the school, one should note that according to Dimbleby his earlier life, with a totally aloof mother and a father who constantly humiliated him in public, had not been a good preparation. Before his last year, as Guardian, at Gordonstoun, he was much happier during an exchange year at Timbertop school in Australia, which was precisely modeled on Hahnian principles in a wild and remote location, and not entirely unlike a prolonged Outward Bound school.

Today the public generally views Hahn's boarding schools in Germany or England as elite. The word can encompass superior scholastic aptitude, but is more likely to conjure, with disapproval, superior parental wealth or aristocratic lineage or personal qualities associated with an idealized image of the latter. Hahn's later total immersion in promoting for all young people the Outward Bound movement and the Award scheme should lay to rest any idea that his sympathies were limited to an elite.

A private school can not survive without a proportion of affluent students, but even at the moment of greatest danger from the Nazi regime Hahn showed his overriding commitment to keeping those whose parents could not pay. In June 1933, when financial panic from the many withdrawals endangered scholarships, he wrote to parents and friends: "The plutocratization has begun. If we continue on this road Salem will lose its reason for existing. Retention and increase in the number of non-paying students is more important than the question of when and whether I may return."

Hahn was often away from Gordonstoun after the war. Others ran the school while he hopped in and out from time to time. A chemistry teacher reports [4] that the second time he had seen the Headmaster he had been teaching for nearly a term. "Who is that man in the hole?" Hahn asked, pointing to him as he worked with students to remove a tree stump. Hahn had then been away for several months in America, Germany and Brown's Hotel.

Hahn had extraordinary success in raising funds and enlisting affluent followers and supporters. A few anecdotes may faintly suggest how Hahn appeared in this capacity. In 1935 a young reporter met with Hahn at Brown's Hotel. The reporter was deeply impressed by Hahn's solemn and deliberate approach, with eyes intently cast down. As he bent from his great height and waited with folded hands before speaking, he sometimes had the mien of priest. Indeed his technique was a form of preaching, but not in the manner of the pulpit. He was argumentative, but fair and never quarrelsome.

Fifteen years later a recruit to Hahn's schemes for the Duke of Edinburgh Award and the United World Colleges describes [4] "innumerable breakfasts in Brown's Hotel. He was a keen introducer. I used to arrive early to try to find out something about the other person but without much hope. We would then be introduced, barely, and Kurt would clasp his hands looking from one of us to the other and saying nothing ... It took me some years to figure out why I sometimes had breakfast in Kurt's room and sometimes in the restaurant, and why in the latter case he seemed to have to absent himself rather often. Of course there was someone more important in his room. Kurt is the only person I have ever met who could handle two separate breakfast parties simultaneously."

Hahn's decade long struggle after the war to establish Outward Bound schools in Germany (by 1949 this had already involved him in ten extended trips to Germany and two to America), modeled on the four week course started in Wales in 1941, can serve as well as any to illustrate the herculean labors that went into all his projects. His first proposal [20] to the Occupation Authorities In 1945 was to immediately establish 100 Kurzschulen (short schools as they were to be called in Germany). His concession to include some vocational part, along with the four-week exposure to education through adventure, did not persuade the authorities, unsympathetic at this time and preoccupied by the Morgenthau plan to dismantle German industry.

In a 1948 visit to the US he next enlisted six prominent citizens to form a Foundation for European Education; the roster included Alan Dulles, Abrahahm Flexner, Christian Herter, the president of Union Theological seminary, as well as the bankers Thomas McKittrick and Hahn's brother in law Eric Warburg. McKittrick introduced Hahn to John McCloy, the American High Commissioner, who was immediately sympahetic and whose wife, Ellen, was later chairwoman of the Foundation.

The Foundation proposed to raise funds for scholarships to Salem and several other boarding schools and to establish three Kurzschulen. But now the German educational hierarchy opposed the plan. It took twenty more years to achieve the goal of three Kurzschulen. Hahn ventured to drop the vocational training part and in 1949 prepared plans for a sea rescue school on the Baltic and a mountain rescue school in the Bavarian Alps, but on a second visit to the US he found that educational leaders and major foundations were now dubious about education through adventure. The Quakers joined in criticizing Outward Bound as reminiscent of the Hitler Jugend, which led Hahn to qualify his admiration for their relief work in Germany by observing that they were showing more concern for pacifism than for peace.

In 1950 Hahn persuaded the Baden Minister of Culture and others to found a sister Foundation for European Education. A conference was held at Gordonstoun, and a guest house established there accommodated nine four-week study groups of German educators from 1951-53. The German foundation was still committed to conventional boarding schools, and used the American funds to support the enrollment of orphans, and children of refugees and resistance fighters. A crack opened in the ice when Hahn convinced a shipowner, who had outfitted two four masted barks as training ships, that the boys should not go to sea without a preliminary training school on land. When the course for eighty boys was held in October 1951, some typical Outward Bound projects were slipped in with the vocational aspect, and the success of this trial, coupled to the raising of German funds to match $ 75,000 from the McCloy foundation, finally led to the opening, in June 1952, of the first German Outward Bound School.

The Weissenhaus sea school soon abandoned any pretense of vocational training, and proceeded with four-week courses for eighty boys, drawn about equally from schools and young apprentices seconded by industry. Chancelor Adenauer proposed a second beach rescue school in Berlin as a demonstration to the Soviets nearby, but the challenge grant from Ellen McCloy was not met. A mountain rescue school in the south was successfully funded in 1956, and 1968 saw a third school established. In 1975 they were back to two when the sea school closed, and after thirteen boys perished in a 1983 avalanche, widespread press accusations of criminal negligence cast a temporary shadow over the mountaineering schools.These schools had 13,000 alumni by 1981 (the most recent figure I have found), despite opposition which has never died in Germany.

"To serve, to strive and not to yield." All over the world young people who have learned to find themselves in mountain solitudes or by experiencing the sea in all its moods have never heard the name of the man who started it all. Once launched by the self-titled midwife, administration of the Outward Bound Schools was in the hands of autonomous Trusts or Committees in each country where they variously flourished. In 1950 Hahn defined the purpose of these schools as being to protect underpriviledged youth against certain ailments of society as he saw them at that time: decay of care and skill, of enterprise and adventure, and of compassion [8]: "Boys or girls, a hundred or so from all walks of life, are gathered in residential courses of one month to practice active citizenship within a self-governing community; to taste vital health as a result of athletic training, to gain self-respect through their surprise at what they can do; to experience (through the sea, the forest, the plains, the rivers or the air) the brotherhood of adventure. In addition there should be some target of proficiency demanding skill and care. Endless variations are possible—practical seamanship; bird-watching; a chapter of contemporary history; mountaincraft; the handling of forestry tools; pre-mining training; bee-keeping; free stone-masonry; horsemanship. Can you really bring about a cure in a month? No, you cannot, but you can in many cases release the cure."

How did it begin? Since the start of the Moray Badge program in 1936, when Gordonstoun's facilities, staff and students had been made available to less affluent boys from the county to involve them in field and track physical training, expeditions, and life-saving, Hahn had been ruminating about how such a training program could be expanded. In the early summer of 1941 he enlisted James Hogan [1], after receiving a miniscule anonymous donation that could support him for three months, to study the feasibility of starting a Badge program in Wales. Every previous appeal to government or foundations for funding had been rebuffed, and recruiting staff seemed impossible in these darkest days of the war when so many teachers had entered the military. But Hahn was undaunted: if there is not enough money to continue studying whether it's feasible, he said, let's just do it and start a permanent residential school now!

In August, when Hahn met the schooner that his students had daringly sailed down from Scotland, a friend and parent who owned the Blue Funnel Shipping Line was with him. Lawrence Holt had found that when his merchant ships were torpedoed the younger seamen were not surviving as well in the small boats as the sail-trained old-timers, and he now proposed to finance a physical plant and supply experienced seamen to staff a sea school at Aberdovey, under Hahn's direction. The school opened two months later, and within a year over a hundred boys were being accepted every four weeks throughout the year. Aberdovey was an Outward Bound rather than vocational school from the start, as merchant marine cadets were joined by boys from industry, from Gordonstoun and some on leave from other schools or about to enter the military, and besides small boat training the curriculum included ahtletic and rescue training, service work and expeditions at sea or accross the mountains. Each course was divided into watches of a dozen boys from different backgrounds, and student officers, who were initially appointed for each watch but could be replaced by member vote after the first week, formed a Court to handle misdemeanours and consult with the staff.

After the war responsibility for the Aberdovey sea school passed permanently from the founders to an independent Trust, and the Outward Bound Movement might have stopped there. But Hahn was again the driving force behind the establishment of a second sea school in 1948, next door to Gordonstoun, which had relocated back to Scotland three years earlier. The first Director describes being hired after a few minutes chat [4]. Hahn picked up the phone in his study and asked the school bursar to send up a note of the funds available to start operations. In a moment a piece of paper torn from the corner of a newspaper arrived on which a modest sum had been inscribed. Glancing at it while holding the telephone receiver in the other hand (the phone rarely stopped ringing), he passed it on and said "Right. Go away and make a Sea School."

By two decades later six British Outward Bound schools had graduated 80,000 boys and girls from some 900 courses. There were every year about as many graduates in the English speaking world as the total recorded to this day by the German Kurzschulen. In the early days students were mostly apprentices from industry which, inconceivable as it seems today, supported the Outward Bound schools as an investment rather than a charity. After the war all British eleven-year-olds took an examination that separated those who would go on to try for a University from those whose vocational education would end at fourteen; most of the latter went into industry as apprentices. As the pay of production workers came nearer to that of supervisors, in the post-war boom, it seemed harder to persuade young men to accept responsibility, and it was imagined that more sophisticated methods of manufacture would justify investment in the quality of the labor force, rather than render it superfluous. By 1957 over 700 different industrial firms had sent boys.

Each Outward bound program was tailored to its milieu. A four-week course was too short to provide the accidents that could allow the "transforming effect of rescue service" to be exercised. The mountain school in the Lake District often had to make do with rescuing sheep. And in schools opened in British colonial territories, in their expiring days, it was quickly evident that adventure for its own sake was inappropriate, and the focus shifted to comunity service.

In America the decade of the fifties was hostile to educational innovation, and enthusiasts for Hahn's ideas could get no hearing. Then, overnight, apathy was transformed into ardent enthusiasm with the advent of the Kennedy administration. In 1961 Miner and several other young Americans who had been exposed to Kurt Hahn's British schools had been vainly knocking on foundation doors for funds for an Outward Bound mountain school in Colorado. Suddenly they found themselves confronted by Sargent Shriver, director of the newly created Peace Corps. After listening to a few words he demanded the immediate establishment of eight Outward Bound schools to train his volunteers. The public did not believe that pampered young people fresh from the classroom would stick it out as ambassadors to impoverished and dangerous lands, and his program dared not risk the fifty per cent drop-out rate usual for overseas employees of federal agencies. Shriver insisted that, since the first volunteers were headed for Africa, their school must be set up in tropical Puerto Rico. He misunderstood Outward Bound in trying to introduce this vocational element; from the beginning it had had to resist the old ingrained idea that it should serve some such specific job-training function. Shriver persuaded the Yale chaplain William Sloane Coffin (soon to gain national prominence as an activist for civil rights and Vietnam draft resistance) to open the camp, and assigned him a former director of Aberdovey to give it authentic Outward Bound character.

Things did not go smoothly with the first class of twelve volunteers. They had been given only two days notice of this final month of training. Only three finished the four-mile run the first day at six AM, and Coffin tried countering mutiny by saying he would recommend that anyone dissatisfied be dismissed from the Corps. But these were not the young respectful Britishers the Aberdovey advisor was used to; they were mature motivated people who wouldn't take orders without knowing why. Flexibility and adaptability were invoked at this point, qualities that would henceforth epitomize the American schools. Coffin discovered that the nearest village needed a deeper well, and improvised a community service alternative on the spot, sending volunteers off to stay and work in remote barrios.

The Colorado Outward Bound school finally opened the following summer, graduating fifty regular students and fifty Peace Corps volunteers destined for Nepal. Industry has never been a source of students in the US. In further contrast to Britain's schools, students were housed in tents, in contrast to the mansions Hahn preferred, and some of the course was at a still more primitive high camp. Physical fitness was promoted by two programs. "Circuit training" involved running around a course with stations for various calisthenic exercises, with each student competing against himself to increase the number of repetitions in a given time. "Ropes courses" were presumably designed ad hoc to provide intimidating as well as strenuous challenges. The Expeditions component at this school would have been into the high mountains, with technical rock climbing. Expeditions at other schools would come to accomodate rivers or salt water or whatever opportunities the site provided. A three-nights solo experience in back country was a new American feature, sometimes featured as a survival school and introduction to edible wild plants, more recently as an experience of solitude and a three-day fast.

Three years and two more schools later, a nationwide avalanche of enthusiasm descended on the Outward Bound staff. Requests for guidance poured in all at once from public school systems, youth clubs, churches, the Naval Academy, Army and Marine Corps, youth detention centers, the Job Corps. Nearly overwhelmed by such demands, the Outward Bound organization gradually settled on a rather ill-defined Outreach Policy, consulting with other institutions and offering training in Outward Bound principles and pactices. Obviously not all such institutions faithfully reflected the original principles, but at least some Outward Bound ideas broke through the barriers to the American educational mainstream. In time a great many public and private high schools came to sponsor some form of outdoor program clearly indebted to Outward Bound.

The American Outward Bound movement has not been as exclusively oriented towards the white middle class as might at first glance appear. Courses for adolescent delinquent boys from detention centers have had some success in reducing recidivism, though this is hard to measure reliably, especially when the authorities hand-pick boys and promise parole if the course is completed. At present only the state of Florida has a specific contract with Outward Bound to provide courses for a large fraction of its juvenile offenders, but there may well be over a hundred programs elsewhere that borrow something from Outward Bound methodology.

Attempts have been made to adapt courses to African-American inner city ghetto boys, and truly heroic efforts have been expended to this end. The challenge is enormous, as my own modest experience suggests. Through the Sierra Club I used to take inner city ten- to fourteen-year-olds on day trips to woods and mountains. There was only one probation officer in Washington DC who would bring his boys out on week-ends. All the boys knew he was also the only white probation officer in the city. None had ever known a father figure. There was nothing in their culture to resonate with "experiencing the brotherhood of adventure through the sea, the forest, the plains, the rivers or the air." Perhaps if Hahn were here today he could meet the challenge these boys and girls presented.

Today there are seven US Outward Bound Schools: two of them are urban centers and the other five run primarilly wilderness courses. By my count 1700 instructors offer about 1000 courses a year, and 300,000 students have succesfully completed these. Overseas 40 schools in 20 countries have graduated another 700,000. Most are still for 16 to 20 year olds. But in the American program there are also courses for all age groups, for family groups, parent and child, couples, mid-life journeyers, life career renewal, managers, courses to develop skills for businesss success, for Viet Nam veterans, children of alcoholics, people with eating disorders, survivors of cancer. A dozen "Urban/Education Programs" add hands-on training to traditional city classroom instruction, and there are special courses for high school drop-outs in trouble with the law or with drugs.

A German critic [9] notes that above all in the US the palette of course offerings has become more and more variegated: as the standards become more relaxed one may question the retention of ties to the Hahnian concept. At the age of 82, Hahn spent two months of 1968 in America, crossing the continent back and forth from Harvard to west coast campuses and from Harlem to Watts, seeking new knowledge about racial tensions and the youthful rebellion then in full force. He was now totally preoccupied with promoting the United World College scheme, but took a keen interest in listening to Miner's briefings on Outward Bound USA. The only concerns he expressed were whether the American schools were giving first aid training its place of honor, and whether some schools might not be so remote in the wilderness that lack of other people might preclude rescue opportunities. In short he seemed captivated by the flexible Outreach policy, so different from what had happened in Britain, and enthusiastic about the innovation of the solo.

From the early days some people of goodwill had criticized Hahn's schools and Outward Bound because qualities they promoted had also been espoused by the Hitler Jugend. For example, a Jewish refugee from Nazi Germany, an old friend who had trained Peace Corps volunteers in the sixties, told me they had quickly stopped using Outward Bound because its program was "completely Nazi!" Responding to these critrics in 1941 [9], Hahn said: "I am afraid we must admit that the young Nazis are expected to be hardened, self-controlled, resourceful and observant. Of their best one might say that they bear all things, endure all things, undertake all things. So does charity, according to the nineteenth chapter of Corinthians. It is nonsense to call [these virtues] either Nazi or Christian." Nonsense, yes, but it was understandable that, at least for a time, there should be a tendency to repudiate personal qualities that had traditionally been considered virtues, after they had been abused for evil ends. For those who characterized specific elements of Hahn's educational program as "fascistoid" after the war, Meissner asked [16]: "Would it not have been possible for members of the deceased Hitler Youth to sail lustily in schooners, to rush about with fire engines, to go over the obstacle course, to do, in fact, everything that seems typical of Gordonstoun, while still beating up Jews and denouncing their parents to the Secret Police?"

There is a more rational and complex side to the "fascistoid" criticism, which notes that some traditional virtues can be enlisted for evil ends more easily than others. A boy more resistant to Nazi ensnarement (or at least less easily recruited) might have emerged from a school that encouraged individualism and resistance to group pressure, instead of conquest of selfish behaviour for the benefit of the community.

Shortly after his return from the last American tour he made at the age of 82 Hahn was hit by a car on a country road near Gordonstoun. The accident, from which he never fully recovered, gave him a new idea. He persuaded Prince Philip (now the Duke of Edinburgh) to support a requirement for first aid training for candidates for drivers' licenses. During the twenty years elapsed since the Outward Bound schools had been securely launched, Hahn's fertile mind had never rested, bringing to life, one after another, a series of related enterprises which can here be only briefly mentioned.

In 1936 Gordonstoun had joined forces with a nearby day school to initiate a County award, the Moray Badge, to be granted for meeting standards in field and track, expeditions, and life-saving. Gordonstoun's athletic facilities and student coaches were made available in the summer to pupils from other schools or boys already at work.The experiment was short-lived, but Hahn never lost sight of the goal of making this non-residential program into a nationwide enterprise with a reach even wider than Outward Bound. After many rebuffs he finally persuaded his former pupil to give his name to the Duke of Edinburgh's Award Scheme. Prince Philip recounts that he fought against sponsoring it for a long time, and it would never have started but for Hahn [18]: "You know what the British are like about that sort of thing. I said I'm not going to stick my neck out ... and everyody saying, 'Ah, silly ass.'"

The leader of the successful Everest Expedition of 1953 tells of Hahn's visit to the Army Staff College the following year to persuade him to be the first Director of the Award Scheme [4]: "I saw approaching the impressive portals a most unmilitary-looking personage clad in a dark cloak and black, broad-brimmed felt hat. My secretary ushered him in. Without ceremony and despite the slightest of previous aquantaince, he advanced on the windows and threw them open, before turning to offer me a limp hand. It was not the most auspicious overture ... but Kurt Hahn's peculiar magnetism cast its spell over me on that grey November afternoon, as the daylight departed and the cold crept in through those open windows."

On this day an educational project that Hahn had planned and promoted for eighteen years came to life. It would grow to affect the lives of far more young people than any other of his projects. Only ten years later about a hundred thousand British boys and girls, ages14-20, (later to 25), were enrolled at any given time in the Award Scheme [21], in which for progressive achievement over the years they could receive the bronze, silver, and finally gold awards. Half came from schools, but industry again contributed substantial numbers, using their own funds and their own staff as adult supervisors. The award was to be granted for achievement in Service, Expeditions, Physical Fitness, and Pursuits and Interests. The latter was an addition to the original County plan. Syllabuses were prepared for two hundred hobby and sports projects in the expectation that technical advances would lead to shorter working hours for everyone. In 1967 the most popular [21] with boys were cycling, fishing and motorcycling; with girls ballroom dancing, reading, soft-toy making, dressmaking and driving. One wonders (but I could not ascertain) which are the favorites today, now that the technical advances have fostered long-term underemployment instead of leisure time.

The real lasting effects which this complex British program yields have not been recently studied, but its current handbook confirms the ever-growing numbers involved: total entrants since inception 2.5 million, awards one million of which 120,000 were gold. The 250,000 enrolled in 1994 contributed 2 million hours of community service. Equally striking 57,000 adult volunteer Mentors have contributed 6 million hours. In view of the vast numbers of adults involved, it is least surprising that Hahn's name should have been forgotten in this program. The Duke of Edinburgh has continued as patron, though he expresses the purpose of the program a bit differently than any one else, as promoting "the art of civilized living." Others tend to speak of "empowering young people to discover new talents, advocate and take action on behalf of others, understand their own strengths and weaknesses, and above all to take responsibility for their own lives."

A process rather than a prize, the program is not competitive and not a youth organization. Participation and choice of project in the four categories is by each young person's initiative. No example could convey the imaginative variety of the 300 that the syllabus suggests under skills and hobbies; several hundred are also suggested for service projects, and for physical recreation and expeditions.

An Award program currently exists in 50 other countries, on a much smaller scale. In 1990 there were 56,000 entrants and 24,000 awards. In 1985 these countries formed a loose association independent from the UK, usually granting the Awards under the name of local head of state or other dignitaries. The "Congressional Award" in the US has perservered on a modest scale for 15 years: in 1994 245 young people earned an award, and the 26 gold award winners were honored with appropriate ceremonies at the Capitol. In some third world countries vocational or even literacy training has replaced skills and hobbies, and in many others where programs started they later surrendered to growing anarchy and civil war. Recent encouraging news is the adoption of the program in France and seven francophone former French colonies.

Toward the end Hahn's interest turned to University education. As mentioned earlier, under the Education Act of 1944 all British eleven-year olds took an examination, on the outcome of which they were divided between vocational and university bound streams. The Outward Bound schools recruited from the vocational stream, who became apprentices in industry after ending their schooling at fourteen. The other stream were eligible for further years of secondary education and, if successful, for competitive University scholarships. University teachers (especially at Oxford and Cambridge) were disappointed with the results; the new students, selected for their skill at cramming factual knowledge and passing examinations, seemed narrow in outlook and interests compared with their "all round" gentlemanly predecessors. Magnates of industry were also unhappy; they were used to recruiting managers at the secondary school level, and the best recruits were now going to University and coming out less malleable. Hahn undertook the complex negotiations that led to the Trevelyan Scholarships [22] financed by industrial firms and intended to select applicants on the basis of character and leadership potential as well as examination skills. From 1959 to 1967 about twenty five of these were awarded each year to students entering Oxford and Cambridge. A review of this experiment shows that these scholars, three quarters of whom had come from elite private schools and would probably have gone to Oxford and Cambridge anyway, did well in academic careers and exclusive areas of the Civil Service (Foreign Office and Treasury), but that not one joined the industrial firms who had paid for the scholarships.

In requiring the candidates to somplete some "special project," however, Hahn had anticipated a problem that still challenges University selection—how to distinguish applicants skilled and motivated only to pass examinations from those with initiative, enthusiasms, determination manifested by long-standing hobbies or skills unrelated to school requirements. But undertaken only to earn the Fellowship, Hahn's projects did not well serve the purpose.

The United World Colleges [23], Hahn's last project, were designed to introduce the principles of Salem to an international student body, in two year residential schools comparable to the senior years of European secondary schools or to American junior colleges. Born from Hahn's friendship with a commandant of the NATO staff college, which brought men from different nations together for military training, the idea was to bring together young people from around the world to promote an understanding which would in time supplant the use of force. The dream was of elite schools whose alumni, like the French *normalien* or the Oxbridge graduate, could pick up the telephone and reach classmates in corridors of power, but now across the world. To the usual challenges of convening distinguished committees and raising funds, there was now added a struggle to gain recognition for an International Baccalaureate, a final exam and diploma that would be recognized by educational authorities and allow application to any university around the world. Anyone entertaining changes in an educational establishment might be forewarned by the immense labors devoted to this till now mostly unsuccessful battle [23]. Hahn's hopes for a college in Germany were thwarted by implacable refusal to accept any substitute for the German Abitur exam; the IB was stigmatized as a possible back-door to university for unqualified kids of rich parents. Rebuffed also in the US when junior colleges and Ivy League prep schools were first approached, the IB was welcomed by public high schools (120 by 1986), where it could counter the senior year apathy that resulted when university admission was determined by scholastic aptitude test at the end of the junior year [the IB degree requires successful completion of a demanding and in some part unique one year course of study.]

The first college opened in Wales in 1962 in a castle restored by Hearst, and amplified by him with medieval buildings collected from far and wide until his attention was diverted to San Simeon. Six years later there were 270 students from 35 countries.The NATO connection had been sucessfully shed, but the desired mix of social classes had not been achieved, and Hahn expressed regret at restricted freedom: uniforms, strict rules about being off campus, and an appointed student council prohibited from discussing matters related to teaching. Along with other principles of Salem, four afternoons each week were reserved for rescue or community service, and craftwork or cultural hobbies. The students were not turning into rootless "world citizens" as some had feared, and it does not surprise me to hear that in the early days the international milieu was actually making some even more conscious of nationality.

There are now eight United World Colleges at scattered locations around the world. All except the agricultural college in Venezuela follow the challenging IB curriculum, with its special supplementary courses on Theory of Knowledge and Conflict Resolution, and all set aside time for community service or outdoor activities related to rescue or environmental studies. The college in New Mexico, opened in 1982 with generous funding by Armand Hammer, currently has 200 students from more than 70 countries.

"Americans love to get worked up over education" according to our current Secretary of Labor Robert Reich in *The Work of Nations* and he adds: "Everyone has views on education because it is one of the few fields in which everyone can claim to have had some direct experience. Those with the strongest views tend to be those on whom the experience had had the least lasting effect." It seems almost every day now that one hears a renewed call for the schools to stand up and rectify all the disasters of a faltering society and economy. The goals Hahn set for his schools were less extravagant. He hoped only to counteract some tendencies he identified in his time toward decline of compassion, physical fitness, care and skill, and enterprise and adventure.

CHAPTER 3

Outward Bound USA Today: Experiments in Inner City Public Schools

In 1995 Hahn's schools are represented in America by four affiliated boarding schools, one United World College, a small Awards Program and seven Outward Bound schools (five "wilderness schools" and two "urban centers"). With their 300,000 alumni, the Outward Bound schools have been the most influential of these institutions, and they have some distinctive features. Outward Bound USA has taken advantage of the vast variety and beauty of our wildernes areas to concentrate on extended, demanding expeditions and the participants requisite physical fitness. These traditional wilderness courses (23 or 26 days) have appealed mostly to the white middle class, but the program has made vigorous efforts to recruit a diverse mixture, by giving talks about Outward Bound in inner city urban schools, and by raising scholarship funds ($1.6 million in 1994).

Hahn's other two goals were service (ideally rescue service where possible), and pursuits and interests. In 1950 [8] Hahn gave a few examples to illustrate the unlimited variety he had in mind for pursuits and interests which might spark a life-long enthusiasm: practical seamanship; bird-watching; a chapter of contemporary history; mountaincraft; the handling of forestry tools; pre-mining training; bee-keeping; free stonemasonry; horsemanship.

These goals could not be fully realized by Outward Bound USA. Service has been represented by readiness for rescue, opportunities to practice which were rare, and by service to each other and to the environment. Introduction to the vast range of possible pursuits and interests envisioned by Hahn was impractical. And if some students did take a lifelong interest in river running or mountaineering from a course, it was not to this end that the schools had introduced them to wilderness adventure. The schools saw adventure not as an end in itself, but as a means, a passageway through which students could discover that they could be more, and could do more in all life's challenges, than they previously believed

And indeed service, and pursuits and interests do seem more at home in Hahn's "Award Scheme," where a young person can spend up to ten years (rather than one month) progressing through the bronze, silver and gold awards. Although miniscule in the US, the Award Scheme in Great Britain (which gives priority to service and to pursuits and interests over Expeditions), has enlisted even more entrants than Outward Bound

The most conspicuously innovative feature In the American one month courses is the "solo," a final three days of fasting in complete solitude. They have also refined "rituals" which make their expeditions more transforming than a first- time wilderness expedition would ordinarily be: quiet periods, group or community circles, inspirational readings at regular intervals, group reflection on learning experiences.

With several major grants from private foundations in the past three years, Outward Bound USA has undertaken a radical experiment to move into the Public School classoom. The current, and I personally think unreasonable, outcry for schools to remedy the growing social and economic decline in America, is mostly following the "back to basics" banner (stressing preparation for college and developing marketable skills). Still, a host of small organizations exist with different agenda, and some of these are actively cooperating with Outward Bound. In 1992 Outward Bound applied for a major grant from the New American Schools Development Corporation, in turn funded by major corporations and, in the following year, by an additional $50 million from the Annenberg gift of $500 million to support "school reform from kindergarten through 12th grade." Their proposal for funding was formulated in principle as a "vision of schools where character and intellect are equally valued, where students learn to take responsibility for their own learning, and where the curriculum sets the content of subject matter in the frame of exciting, interdisciplinary 'learning expeditions,' which may occupy eight to ten weeks of classroom time." The plan was to transform existing schools, or start new ones, at sites initially chosen to be in Boston, New York City, Portland [Maine], Dubuque and Denver (as of January 1996 Memphis, Cincinnati and San Antonio have been added to the list). Among grant applications simultaneously submitted, Ouward Bound's was among the two per cent to be funded.

In the Twenties, Hahn had given thought to introducing the principles and practices of Salem to a day school, but had concluded it was impractical. The kind of school Hahn was considering would have been a Gymnasium all of whose middle class students were university bound. And of course here, as in his boarding schools, Hahn would not have intervened in the classroom, where a conventional curriculum would have been delegated to a subordinate "director of studies." In contrast,

Outward Bound today is going all out into the classrooms of inner city schools, whose Afro-American, Hispanic and other kids come from an underclass to whom everything about "schools" is often not only meaningless but demeaning. I have found it insults one of these twelve-year-olds when I ask if he plays on any school athletic team. He plays on a street team!

My information about the radical move into the Public School classroom in the past three years comes mostly from Outward Bound's grant applications, reports and preliminary teachers' manuals. The methods being adopted to reform Public Schools and realize their goals are so varied, intense and tentative that I can not hope to give any balanced summary here. I can only comment briefly, first on new teachers, then on new schools

NEW TEACHERS. About 4000 teachers, mid-life and beginners, had undergone some form of training by 1993, in what Outward Bound calls "Expeditionary Learning." Some have simply gone on a typical wilderness expedition for a week or longer. Others have attended one to ten-day workshops, where in small groups they develop curriculum proposals and gain experience in what will be communal classrooms with groups of teachers and students planning and working together. Each day begins with a game or problem-solving initiative, stressing communication and creative tension. Outward Bound rituals are woven into the workshops, stressing the value of the individual and the effectiveness of the team. Small groups then focus on developing curricula based on possible "Urban Expedition" topics.

An Urban Expedition, which may last several months, will relate to anything relevant to the lives of the students, and to places and institutions in their locality, and may redefine itself, as it proceeds, by initiatives of both teachers and students. It is hoped it will develop so as to include experience relating to most standard curriculum subjects. Math has been found to be an exception, which must be taught in the old-fashioned way, but writing, the arts, social sciences usually find a niche. Here are a few samples of the kinds of Expedition topics proposed: Geology (using *Tom Sawyer* as text, because much time would be spent on cave exploration); Japan; Independence; Revolution; Law and Justice; local senior citizens; local store owners; a novel about people lost in a cave; "Our City, Ourselves" (focus: how can we tell when a community is thriving?); pond life, water; urban renewal; endangered species." A teacher may need several months for planning once such a topic has been chosen.

NEW SCHOOLS. The schools will be "family-focused," providing access to necessary support services and empowering distressed families to seek help before a problem becomes a crisis. Community engagement will be built into the design of every learning expedition: participating experts may be an architect, a biologist, a long-distance truck driver, an immigrant grandmother

By November 1994 some Expeditionary Learning Program was in place in schools in at least ten locations. Two schools are totally new. The Rocky Mountain School, created by pooling resources from 4 public school districts, features several unique administrative features, including direction by three "lead teachers," multi-age grouping of students, and extended blocks of time for both classroom and out-of-school projects. The "School for the Physical City" (described in detail later) was established in September 1993 in New York City in collaboration with several like-minded organizations. At the next level are four "transformed" existing schools, all in Dubuque. In "phased-in" schools transformation is planned to be spread out over a period of time.It is worth noting this program's success in a Portland Regional Vocational Center. Formerly a dumping ground for at-risk kids, it is now sought-after by parents. Finally there are "Spirit of Expeditionary Learning" schools which, through contacts with Outward Bound, implement expeditions on a smaller scale.

I have chosen to descibe in a little more detail the new "School for the Physical City" in New York City, because I have the advantage of an outsider's report in a *New York Times* article (May 28, 1995) which Outward Bound has reprinted in a volume of news clippings. On her first visit, the reporter found no one at the school. Half were on a field trip to Harriman State Park, and the others were scattered over Williamsburg Bridge, studying its redesign. Opened in September 1993 in collaboration with the Board of Education, Cooper Union, and the New York Mission Society (with its 2000 acre upstate camp site), the school occupied a few fugitive empty classrooms in the leviathan hull (the typical New York School accomodates 4000) of an existing middle school. Two days before opening, the nine-person staff somehow scrounged some furniture and basic supplies, not overlooking a large trash pile in the school's courtyard. Initially there were about 150 students from 6th, 7th, and 9th grades (small was considered indispensable) but despite some hope for mentoring by the higher class, it was soon replaced by an 8th grade. (To keep some perspective, we might note that New York City currently budgets $8 billion for one million public school students and their 65,000 teachers)

There is no tracking or segregation of handicapped or gifted students. The 6th to 8th grades are intermingled, and there are no failures. This is indeed from Hahn—each is judged by his or her improvement from wherever they started. There are two 90-minute periods, morning and afternoon, and in between a few electives such as French, poetry, and tutorials in English and math. The morning begins with a group pursuing a specific project, sitting in a half-circle and discussing the reading they had done at home the night before. The teacher asks questions (most students have never been asked to speak in a classroom before and may be put off at first), and then if no expedition outside the school is planned, the teacher talks about additional new materials relating, in the widest sense, to the class's topic. Sometimes there is an invited guest lecturer.The period ends with students writing in their journals, and five minutes of silent, collective reflection.

"Kites in the Wind: How do They Fly?" was the semester topic of a former mechanical engineer. While building kites for 3 months the students delved into properties of the atmosphere, aerodynamics, use of protractors, Bernoulli's principle, with some use of Cooper's computers and the 2000 acre upstate campsite. In Hudson River Park the day before Christmas, the various models were put to the test and their behaviors analyzed. Throughout the term kids, some of whom had literally never written a word on paper before, took notes, kept journals, wrote stories—even a newspaper.

At year's end the school had one of New York's highest attendance records, 94.5 percent of students present on an average day, and despite a moratorium on building it had aquired its own home in five stories of a newly renovated former department store.

The ongoing ill-tempered complaints about the Public Schools, and the irresponsible claims that they are the cause of, and must rectify, the country's social and economic decline, are topics beyond my horizon. Let's hope these ambitious experiments of Outward Bound USA will have some permanent impact on all our Public Schools and their 50 million students. What would Hahn have thought of the decision to focus on a middle school and the age group 12 to 14? Hahn focused on the age group from 14 to 19, believing these adolescent years to be the crucial ones for character development, and though some of his principles and practices were followed in his junior schools, they were designed for the older group to which his personal interest was confined. Now under circumstances as different as night from day it seems just possible that the fortuitous choice of a middle school may be propitious. Far ahead of their contemporaries in the basics of reading and writing, and one hopes also in math, these students may enter high school with enough self-esteem, responsibility, enthusiasm for knowledge and hope for their futures to sustain them in a culture where the age of thirteen marks a rite of passage to pregnancy, drugs and firearms.

Some letters of recent graduates of the traditional one month courses may illustrate more graphically what student experiences are actually like. Steve Truitt, from the "Harvard/Outward Bound Project in Experience-Based Education at the Harvard Graduate School of Education," sent me a few from younger alumni, from which the following short excerpts are taken.

From an 18-year old girl: "Have just finished a ten-mile run through the desert.... It is here in Utah that I finally feel whole.... I learned more about myself than I knew I could."

Another young girl on a whitewater raft trip: "Behind an Outward Bound experience there is always a story to tell. It is impossible to explain to someone who has never been there. It is hard to understand that feeling when you think you have given all the strength and heart possible, and you are proven wrong by a river."

From a young school teacher: "Whether it was a group problem solving initiative like 'Acid River,' an individual challenge like rock climbing, or the daily task of hiking and setting up camp, [the activity] was completely absorbing. Accomplishing each day's goals required a great deal of commitment to the group ... continuing to walk despite exhaustion, continuing to climb despite fear, or remaining supportive and patient with 'slower' and 'weaker' members.... It was clear to me during the course that people can do more than they and others think they can."

From a young father rafting on the Green River with his son: "The beauty of the surroundings enhanced the whole process.... Key to the entire experience, though, was our interaction with the Outward Bound staff. They were remarkable!... Their combined efforts produced an experience which I will not forget for a long time to come."

From a young man interested in becoming an instructor: "Just returned from a 23-day Leadership Alpine Mountaineering course.... In the beginning there were 38 of us and all the faces were quiet, unfamiliar and scared.... Some sabotaged their equipment to get out and others faked injuries. Started with a 2-week training phase for low impact or "leave no trace" camping as a group, wilderness first aid, and most importantly how to live in the woods with 10 complete strangers. Then two weeks of backpacking with 60 pound packs. I learned about the principles of enterprising curiosity, tenacity in pursuit, undefeatable spirit, sensible self-denial and respect and compassion for myself and others. The greatest gift of all it has given me a purpose for living again."

And finally excerpts from letters about wilderness expeditions which Greg Farrell [Outward Bound Vice-President for Urban and Education Programs, and Chief Executive Officer of the Expeditionary Learning Project] has collected from older participants who have had prior experience as educators.

From a staff member in "Managing Education Change:" "I shall never forget the tranquillity and majesty of the canyons and rivers, my 'solo' with a green apple and a sleeping bag, the flash flood on the way to the pictoglyphs, the night run to the last camp, the importance of cooperation and teamwork.... You have designed a marvelous program, a true learning experience."

From a director of the "Partnership for Effective Education Management:" "My week on Penobscot Bay and Hurricane Island was one of the richest educational experiences of my life. When I was walking the wire and Laura told me to let go of the rope that supported me 30 feet in the air, I could not think how to solve the problem of remaining on the wire. [Principle One: Give students something important to work on!]. But I finally had to let go, lunged for the next rope in the sequence, and hung on. [Principle Two: Having presented the problem, give students the time and tools to discover the answer for themselves; it will stick!].... Expeditionary Learning is the real thing."

From a professor in the Harvard Graduate School of Education: "The trip down the Green River was a great experience. The important impacts for me are a sharp increase in my desire to be exposed to natural beauty and to the kind of challenge incorporated in your expeditions. I think you have a powerful technique but that the trick is to figure out ways to reach many more students at lower costs."

From a lecturer at NYU Law School: "The Hurricane Island course was intense. Rowing through Felix's swells; belaying our convoy-mates as they climbed through rocks and ropes; rapelling for the first time in my life; leaning, balancing, swinging, climbing, squirming, teetering, bouncing and zipping through the ropes course—the intensity focused my mental and physical abilities on each task.... The weaving together of intense experience and quiet reflection was particularly effective.... I think I learned more about teaching than about anything else."

From a Superintendant of Schools in Maine: "I have to tell you that [Hurricane Island] was one of the highlights of my life.... I could fill volumes explaining why this experience has had such a profound effect. One reason is how I see public education incorporated with your program. We must, however, be creative in funding such experiences."

The letters give some student impressions of the programs and "rituals" of the traditional short courses. Specifically for the new experiments in the Public Schools, Outward Bound USA has additionally compiled a set of principles, listed here in an Appendix on pages 153-4.

A Salem Diary: The Senior School; May to July 1933

This and the following chapters will tell the story of the defiant strategies by which Hahn's German schools survived the thirteen years of Nazi rule, as reconstructed alternately from my own diary as a 13-year-old, while I was there during the first year, and from the school archives. Arrested soon after Hitler seized power on Jan 31st 1933, Hahn had escaped to England and founded there, as we have seen, a remarkable series of educational projects.

Since Hahn will seldom be present henceforth, except in memory, what follows will be a different story; in part it will serve as an honest account of everyday life in a small community that opposed the Nazi regime. But I think this episode at Salem should also have some place in any memoir of Hahn. It was there, and probably also during the many years before 1920 when he was planning to start the school, that all the basic principles were developed that later flowered in England and around the world. Now we will see how these principles fared under the worst conceivable circumstances.

On May 9th my parents delivered me to Spetzgart, high above the shores of the Bodensee, a senior school (for ages 13 to 18), and enrolled my brother Sean, four years younger, at the nearby junior school at Hohenfels. My diary begins:

> *There are quite a few schools around here all under the same management. One, the biggest, is called Salem and has about 400 boys. The next is Spetzgart where I am which has 100 and then there is Hohenfels which is for the smaller boys and not very big. There may be more but those are all I know. In Spetzgart there are six grades, Unter—and Oberterzia, Unter—and Obersecunda, and then the highest are the Unter—and Oberprimas. The school of Spetzgart is in two buildings, one new and the other old. Which however have been built together like this: [an L-shape]. Then aside from that*

there are a Schlosserei [metal craft shop], a Schreinerei [carpenter shop], a garage, a big barn for hay and some other smaller edifices. There are some very nice pieces of wood furniture and the stairs are all carved out in the old building. The girls building I don't know much about." (Girls are almost entirely ignored by the young adolescent author.) *"In the boys wing, on the bottom or basement are the Schuhputzraum [where arduous shoe polishing takes place every day], the Kitchen and the furnace or Heizung, on the next the dining room, the shower and locker rooms, the Glass Halle, some classrooms and the art room. On the third floor are the living room, more classrooms and the boys' and Lehrer's rooms, on the next where I am there are nothing but boys' living rooms. On the top are the Punchen place, the place where all beginners in music practice and most of the others by request, the Zeichenen Saal and the servants' rooms.*

Spetzgart is situated in hilly farmland some distance above the lake, out of sight of the nearest peasant village, surrounded by ploughed fields, orchards and pasture, and backed by steep grassy meadows and fir woods. Today I think of the similar farmland where I now live in Maryland as among the most beautiful in America. But when I went to Spetzgart I was unimpressed. At that time my "grande passion," as Hahn puts it, was to return to my homeland in Carmel on the California coast.

How I came to be at Spetzgart had something to do with parental notions about the importance of learning foreign languages. A writer who could work any place, and at a time when there still lingered an impression that the brightest Americans were in Paris, my father chose to spend two years traveling in Europe. The first year Sean and I had spent in a Swiss boarding school, where the English speaking students were segregated and taught entirely in English. My parents may have chosen Salem because it was rather well known in England. But when I arrived, after Hahn's arrest, a flourishing exchange program [24] had diminished. Amidst German boys I learned the language there sink or swim fashion, to the level of a schoolboy vocabulary, rather quickly. Never having "studied" German in the 60 years since, I hope this early exposure plus my now dog-eared dictionary have rendered the translations in this book reasonably acceptable. In May 1933 the school was no doubt anxious to replenish its diminishing foreign students (many German parents were also soon to withdraw their children), and I expect my credentials were not closely questioned. The diary describes my admission:

First we went up to talk to the lady principle who said all about how healthy it was etc. and I got my lessons vaguely arranged.

For the afternoon I was put into the charge of Dennis, the only other American boy, a few years older than I, who

> *showed me the shops and all the rest of the school. His father is a writer, and he is bringing up his son to be the same apparently. He can typewrite the touch system good and fast, do stenography very fast and he takes a whole lot of magazines and newspapers.*

Before the day was over I was detached from the illusory safety of this American redoubt, and immersed in a strange new life.

> *It was awfully strange at first but it isn't so bad afterwards. There is one big washing room with a lot of showers and basins that you turn upside down to empty and right next to it there is a big dressing room where you keep all your clothes in lockers and right near that is a big shoe room. I am in a room of five including myself, one of them is the captain of all the juniors and naturally this room's captain. Every room even if it has only two people in it has one captain. I am in with the three juniors I like the best. We had supper quite early and then the captain insisted I was very tired and thus I went to bed. The pillow is only a little bit of straw with a cover but then that comes from being the last. The boy I go around with the most is Jobst Frowein, as Dennis is a senior although he ought not to be and I don't see so much of him.*

My room-mates and friends were all in the Oberterzia, the class ahead of mine. There were only two other boys and three girls in the Unterterzia and one of the boys was Nikolaier, with whom I would soon find myself on bad terms. Jobst remained my best friend throughout the year at Spetzgart, and is the only German boy identified by first name in the diary. In fact, five monhs later I had to enlighten the diary reader:

> *Frobst, Frowein, Jobst, Jobele and Froschbein are all the same person.*

Regarding classwork:

> *I am taking Latin here and I hate it. Also Mathematics, drawing designs, making big letters in ink, Biology, Religion, German Literature and now German alone with Fräulein Ewald's mother. Fräulein Ewald is the head lady, Herr Wutsdorf the head teacher, Herr Siegrest for German and Latin, Fräulein Unverricht to buy books from and Fräulein Rokol who signs all the notices and must do something else. There are two* Schwesters *(nurses) but only one*

> *does any Schwestering. They also have a very good and fancy place for sick ones with two rooms as informitory [sic]. The English boy who is called Jocelin Young is up now but of course his (broken) arm is still in a sling.*

The diary record of the first week dwells at more length on some of the non-academic "other activities" programs.

> *The first morning I had to do the* Dauerlauf *with the rest which is a run at six o'clock. After that you have to wash once or twice and then breakfast. Then after some lessons there was a* Waldlauf *(cross-country run) and then we had to wash several times again. After lunch we had blacksmithing and I worked on an idea of my own which was making a knife which was curved all the way around.*

Another afternoon when a volkerball game was rained out

> *we had to have a* Waldlauf *instead, despite great protests and threatenings of a Terzia strike. For a* Waldlauf *all you are allowed to wear is tennis shoes and short pants. Dennis says it is the same in winter when it is snowing. We had a lot of fun with the senior in charge and walked every time he stopped looking. Then a bunch of us including me who had been making the most trouble had to run way off while the rest ran back. We did run and on the last part pretty fast too.*

These long distance runs one or more times a day must have seemed a distinctive feature of Salem, long before jogging became fashionable, and the benefits are suggested by a parenthetic diary entry two weeks into the term:

> *The boys here certainly look more healthy than any that ever came from Montana (the Swiss school) and I may be wrong but it seems to me that they look healthier and healthier as they were here longer and longer.*

The part of the curriculum that I liked best could be catalogued as planned and ad hoc "adventures." The first diary entry records a Fox and Hound hunt where I was a chaser; the foxes eluded us despite much racing about muddy hillsides. Saturday afternoons were dedicated to Innungs.

> *I joined up for map making because I didn't undertand any of the others and you have to map all the country around here with correct distances and heights. After supper one boy had found a crow's nest way up in the top of a tree and the Englishman, Mr. Chew, had*

climbed up a nearby tree and lassoed one of the branches. Thus there was a rope coming down and they had brought along pulleys so everyone could get up. I was the last one to go up in the swing. It is really only about thirty feet high but when you get up there it looks several thousand feet down. It was getting dark but after climbing up branches a lot higher I could still plainly see the nest. It was absolutely full of baby crows.

Mr. Chew, who years later became headmaster of Gordonstoun school in Scotland, was a rather remote figure to me, who was usually out sailing with the senior boys on the lake, where he had his own imposing boat, the Godenwind. There was a rest or "liegen" period after lunch:

My mentor or the man in charge of me is Mr. Chew, the English master here. He reads mystery stories most of the time and one day he read something out of San Michele which was interesting to me because I saw the villa on the island of Capri.

Mr. Chew resigned on July 12th at a stormy faculty meeting, at which the new director Meese announced that no criticism would be allowed of his descisions, and anyone violating this would be discharged without notice.

The staff member I most admired was Herr Wutsdorf, a generation older than Mr. Chew, who directed sailing for the younger boys, for whom he perhaps felt more affinity.

The head man of the school or the man who has charge of the sailing and boys in general was a submarine captain in the war. He is very tough and not very strong looking and all the smaller boys are afraid of him.

But three weeks later:

Herr Wutsdorf doesn't seem nearly so fierce any more as when I first came and anyway he likes me quite well, very different from his attitude to Dennis. When he heard Dennis was leaving the next day he said 'Gott sei dank.'

My thirteenth birthday came up ten days after my arrival and my room captain Bernard Buhl gave me a book, "Der Rote Kampflieger," about the career of the fighter pilot ace von Richthofen. I remember the book well to this day, and even better the remarkable fact of the gift. Anyone who remembers high school in the US (or for that matter probably any place else) will recognize this as uncharacteristic of the relationship between a senior and a seventh grader. At the time I was shamefully lacking in gratitude.

The Spetzgart school in 1930 and (clockwise): Marina Ewald, Maria Köppen and Robert Chew (in later years as headmaster of Gordonstown).

Bernard is pretty silly about all the juniors and has yellow hair and always wears glasses. He got very excited when I put a plug in one of the holes which has not got the wires properly covered and made a short circuit which put out all the lights on the whole floor and it was many hours later they were fixed.

I did not appreciate his need, in his last year, to study for the fateful Abitur exam, at the same time that he was counsellor to all the junior boys, and he might justifiably have felt in need of sanctuary from my harrasment. At the alumni homecoming holiday on June 3rd I wrote:

Bernard left early in the morning for the whole three days I believe and his sister came to get him in a very fancy car.

From the school archives I have a list of "Helpers" appointed by Fräulein Ewald for this term. After "Guardian," underlined at the top, I see in descending order House Helper, Work Helper, Sport Helper, Watersport Helper, Helper for Intellectual Matters, Day Student Helper and then, next to Girl Helper at the bottom of the hierarchy, Bernard Buhl Junior Helper. The diary mentions the Guardian only once, as captain of a Cutter the first time I went sailing. The color-bearers, who were self-selected in contrast to the helpers, are also mentioned by name only once, on June 15th:

In summer their water supply which comes from springs begins to get very low and we all have to bathe in the lake (instead of showers). The lake gets shallow so you have to go out quite a long ways. One of the senior Farbentragers *goes out in a row boat and you have to keep just behind it.*

However, frequent reference to "captains" supervising running and other sports and adventures confirms that these senior students were fulfilling roles of junior faculty, or what we might think of now as benevolent summer camp counsellors.

In my own experience of other schools the attitudes of seniors to younger students have been a bit more likely to be characterized by bullying than by sympathetic concern. When Hahn began to introduce the Salem system to British boys at Gordonstoun, a teacher there noted [1] that Hahn was ever "vigilantly on the lookout to bring schoolboy incidents of bullying or mob justice into the open and use them as opportunities for education. Hahn, good schoolmaster that he is, has never been fearful of repetition; it is significant that as headmaster of Gordonstoun he had an almost obsessive preoccupation with the Parable of the Good

Samaritan.The desire to have it read to the school seemed to seize him again and again."

In my first participation in what was called "*Wehrsport*" the younger boys at Spetzgart challenged Hohenfels to a match that involved trying to tear off the enemy's armbands while keeping one's own. I borrowed a bicycle for the ride over, which involved some tube patching by the senior Captain. Hohenfels won and got all of our bands while we got only two of theirs, including Sean's. *Wehrsport* played a much bigger role in the next term at Spetzgart. Hahn had introduced some military drill after the French occupation of the Ruhr in 1923, and after 1930 allowed boys to participate in the youth camps for "military sports" organized by the Stahlhelm, a right wing organization of World War I veterans. I will use the German word as "paramilitary training" exaggerates the battlefield orientation of some of these exercises. For example, here is an account in the school records for October 11, 1932 of a *Grosses Kriegspiel* held under the direction of Herr Meese. "The half-island between Bodman and Dingelsdorf represented Formosa. Our girls under the leadership of Frl. Ewald were a group of English Ladies who had been captured by Chinese pirates. Two Cutters with sea cadets were dispatched to rescue them. They succeeded to bring most of the girls off in the Cutters but unfortunately through an oversight the pirates had been launched too late and had little chance to capture the Ladies."

Some *Wehrsport* exercises even during my first term were a bit more militaristic than the one just described. On May 27th:

> *After supper everyone had to march down to Überlingen and watch the parade there as it is Stahlhelm day. All the Hitler troops of this school had to wear their uniforms. It seemed like there were more soldiers than people from this litle city. It was very very impressive of the power of Germany. They have the young Hitlers and the young Stahlhelms who were indeed very young and who also marched around and also they had a large troop of girl Hitlers who could sing well but nothing else.*

A memorandum in the Salem archives [24] notes that on this day a Nazi youth leader had given a speech (of which I must have been unaware) to staff and students in the Spetzgart courtyard, "ruling on everything. The school marched that evening in formation to the Stahlhelm festival. (It was) interesting that students who would previously have thought it beneath their dignity suddenly joined in singing the patriotic songs."

My impression of Germany's growing military power are at odds with the message in many clippings from German news media pasted in the diary, which outdo each other in demonstrating Germany's weakness compared to that of the neighbouring countries. A typical example is an illustrated tabulation cut from a newspaper in November, which appears next to a photo of Hindenburg at the ballot box exhorting the German people to back Chancellor Hitler. The table lists arms for France and Germany, respectively, as follows: troops, 700,000 and 100,000; tanks, 2500 and 100; heavy artillery, 1200 and 20; machine guns, 37,000 and 2,000; planes, 5000 and 0. This theme was fequently expounded in the classroom. My memories of Geography class are that it was virtually confined to maps of the provinces lost after the war. Sentiments of melancholy and peace-loving outrage accompanied the frequent invocations of the lost "Elsass" and "Lothringen."

Neither the diary nor the contemporary school archives note a striking event that occured only one day after my arrival, the infamous book burning of May 10th. But at least some Spetzgart students did participate, as I learned from a report prepared by seniors at Salem to commemorate the 50th anniversary of Hahn's arrest [25]. The reporters took pride in having found proof that a majority of their forebears had held to their ideals under the heavy pressure of the Nazi hate campaign, in the fact that "on 10th May 1933 they put the books of the 'proscribed poets' in the covers of their old maths and physics books, put them back in the bookcases, and took the cashiered maths and physics books to the funeral pyre directed by the regime in Aufkirch." As a retired scientist, who has spent 45 years doing laboratory research in chemistry and biology, I must excuse myself for feeling only lukewarm enthusiasm for this evidence of student idealism. When the student report was presented to an audience of friends and alumni some of the latter found it hard to understand Hahn's later release of alumni from the injunction of his circular letter of 1932. The student reporters did not answer these questions but were prepared to sidestep them: "We saw in this the same dilemna in which the catholic church found itself. Having threatened all Nazi followers with excommunication before 1933, after 1933 they tacitly withdrew the threat, as it was now a question of the government party in power. Also Hahn saw clearly that under these altered circumstances he would have put his friends and students in a position of unbearable conflict."

A diary entry quoted earlier in this chapter mentioned an English boy recovering from a broken arm. Jocelin is the same Jocelin Winthrop-Young who welcomed my wife and me and introduced me to the archives at Salem sixty years later. The diary reports:

Jocelin has some very good rock climbing pictures of himself, family and Mr. Chew whom he has known for years, long before he came here. His father (mentioned at the end of Chapter 1) *used to be about the best in England until he lost one of his legs.*

Jocelin was an improvisor of games. One was for one of us to go ahead and blaze a tree every now and then, and then the other would have to follow without the first one seeing the one that was tracking. Another was to find a good bank and then make roads in it. Another day after working for a little while on the roads we had a war. The object was for one of us to hold a fort which was up on a bank against the other one by throwing clods of dirt. This day after supper was the time to get pocket money and mine was supposed to be two marks. However I inveigled four marks out of Herr Wutsdorf and almost 50 pfennigs more.

Earlier in this chapter I noted that the part of the curriculum I liked best was the planned and ad hoc adventures, but perhaps I need to qualify the "ad hoc." The fox and hound hunt and the war game against Hohenfels seemed to develop on the spur of the moment but they had presumably been designed by the staff. It was an English boy who was really initiating ad hoc games, and it was the English master Mr. Chew who conceived the truly ad hoc adventure of roping up to the crow's nest. This could fairly be put in the ledger of passive German submission to authority that is associated with the terrible years ahead, but I think it also warrants reflection on possible shortcomings of Hahn's educational ideas.

My English friend Jocelin excelled at field and track. In the Salem curriculum a morning break was set aside four times a week for these exercises, in which each student was competing only against his own previous record. Jocelin's best event was the high jump, and I have a vivid memory of one incident connected with this. The high jump had very special signficance for Hahn. In a scrapbook prepared to enlist support for the opening of Gordonstoun [3] he wrote: "We lay great stress on the athletic training of those who are not naturally keen nor particularly gifted in sports. The high jump, for example, is specially fitted to develop power of decision. The boy of refined intellect and high sensitiveness often shrinks from this test in the beginning, and inasmuch as he overcomes his aversion to gathering up his strength, the life of action begins to attract him. We know of cases of stammerers who have been greatly benefited by the high jump."

One afternoon I joined Jocelin when he was practicing the high jump by himself. The bar was first placed way up, and then way down again, and I was feeling quite embarrassed to be practicing with this track star. At one point I must have gotten over a level at which it had so far been repeatedly knocked down, and Jocelin stopped and emphatically congratulated me. I was taken aback, telling him "Come on, you're the school champion," and so on. He would have none of this and rebuked me sharply, repeating the congratulations. My gaining an inch was more important than his being the champion. I think what has helped anchor the memory is a sense that I have listened for sixty years and never seem to have heard this again. The memory has stood for my encounter, perhaps in that troubled year my principle encounter, with the "Salem system." After Salem I spent three years at an excellent American secondary school where, in accord with common practice, the only accepted subdivision of society was into winners and losers. I found that I was in the bottom ten per cent at baseball and soccer, and quickly learned to affect an appropriately disdainful attitude to competitive games.

This episode might have been a lesson as well as an encounter. But I have never passed it on; Salem seems to have had no influence on my character. Might it have had? Perhaps with five consecutive years in normal times, but during the one year I was there I seem to have favored the role of trouble making rebel.

At this point a personal note about the very first of my many boarding school experiences can help explain my adoption of this role. I was five and my brother was one at the time of the first family tour abroad, and the story was that I had taken to throwing up and not eating after he was born, and was alarmingly skinny on arrival in Paris, where an eminent local phsysician urged my parents to place me in a sanitorium in the Swiss Mountains. On arrival there I cried until my mother promised to come back the next day, but she did not do so. When she did return five months later she found me playing with a "bateau de vapeur" which I could not name in English, but the nutritional problem persisted until it was finally cured by an appendectomy five years later, possibly one of the more successful outcomes of psychosurgery on record.

Jocelin, along with Mr. Chew, departed at the end of the term, and both of them migrated to Gordonstoun when it opened in Scotland. It is time to turn to another topic.

Ten days after my arrival I wrote the following:

> *There are still however quite a few Jews in this school and they are sure the worst boys here, sometimes I think Hitler wasn't so dumb.*

Evidently this must reflect antisemitic talk going around among the boys, although I don't recall such among my friends, nor any indoctrination from the staff until the following term with the arrival of Nazi Kommissar Flierl. However, I also do not recall any hint of criticism of Hitler from the staff during a period when the archives show that some of them were being denounced by colleagues and students for opposing the new regime. I would have known the word "Jew" only from reading; I had never heard anyone in my family circle identified either as being a Jew or as being a *goyim*. The realization that Jews could be a socially distinguishable group or a vehicle for prejudice in America came only when I entered Harvard college four years later. An article in the Bodensee Rundschau of June 3rd, emphasizing that the job was not finished with Hahn's departure, claimed [3] that Salem students were mostly sons of feudal aristocrats and rich Jewish capitalist, and that there were still twenty to thirty Jews enrolled. During my year at Spetzgart I identified only two boys as Jewish. Strauss was a sensitive and awkward boy; Nikolaier was the antithesis. The latter I described as

> *the dumbest boy by far in the lowest class (my class in fact) and awful at athletics, all he does in fact is to walk around with his hair all combed and his hands in his pockets singing songs." The last reference to Nikolaier is at the end of the term: "After supper there was the first school dance. It wasn't very exciting or anything like an American party as they were all so terribly careful to be etiquitique [sic]. Aside from the Jews only the older boys danced and the older girls. Nikolaier danced quite a lot.*

The charge of "awful at athletics" does not mesh with a memory of Nikolaier at the tennis net, dropping a fast return at waist level so that it bounced out of play only inches on the other side, nor does it seem compatible with an account of a boxing match with Nikolaier:

> *After tea I went up to Jocelin's room to read a book and after a while Nikolaier came in and said he wanted to fight. In the first round I nearly knocked him out as he wasn't expecting anything. Then for the second round he went off to fetch Teo for his referee, and Jocelin explained that we would only spar sort of this time. However he didn't take it that way and as he is really a fairly good boxer and I am not it was with him. He hit me once under the eye where it started bleeding and so it stopped right away. He broke Teo's arm fighting with him several days before about which there had been a terrible row and anyway boxing is forbidden. We had to tear out and go for a little walk; luckily [for him] it didn't swell up much and after about an hour we came back and no one noticed.*

Aside from the self-serving note by an author who usually lost fights he could not back out of, the contrived quality of this fight can be accounted for by the tradition of boxing at Salem. Hahn had instituted formal boxing matches, two rounds carried out in his room, to settle disputes or as a punishment. Golo Mann describes such a match [13], after he and another boy had been charged with improperly tying up and ridiculing an opponent during a war game. That evening an announcement was posted in the dining hall that they would box because of "crude and cowardly behaviour." Hahn deliberated with the seconds after the match, and announced the winner, as well as whether they had fought with courage. Evidently by my time, ten years later, Frl. Ewald was discouraging this tradition. The debate over the preservation of traditions continues to this day. The current Markgraf, grandson of the founding Prince Max, feels that the school has forsaken its traditions and plans to terminate its lease at Salem. In replying to this criticism the current director recently singled out these same boxing matches as the foremost example of a tradition that would be unthinkable today [5].

It seems that when I wrote that Jews were the worst boys in the school, and Hitler wasn't so dumb, what I had in mind when I wrote "Jew" was actually Nikolaier. But obviously prejudice is defined as soon as the name of a community is substituted for the name of an individual. Perhaps I would have been less susceptible if adults had discouraged hostile generalizations about the Filipino underclass at home. I doubt it; a thirteen year old not susceptible to prejudice sounds a bit unreal, even alarming. Happily, Nikolaier escaped. When my family and I stopped between terms at the Swiss school I'd earlier attended, I noted:

> *Who should I see but my old friend Nikolaier whom the Nazis chased out of Germany.*

My "anti-semitism" vanished the moment I was separated from the peers who had promoted it, but perhaps a humble homily is appropriate before leaving this topic. The consensus is that anti-semitism remained quite shallow in Germany, outside the small ranks of Nazi fanatics. Hitler's hope that shared hatred of the Jews would unite the Volksgemeinschaft and assuage the occupied countries of Europe was in vain. The holocaust then teaches that prejudice, any prejudice at all, should be constantly fought against. I am looking now at such a prejudice of mine, a minor one among others, but persistent. It is a momentary prejudgement at the first instant of encountering any German that says yes, this person will confirm that the Holocaust could only have occurred in Germany.

Now I must return to various aspects of school life, first classroom studies and then: service work, music and drama, craftwork, sailing adventures on the Bodensee (which most captured my enthusiasm) and finally the rare occasions when behind the scenes conflicts with the Nazi regime broke into my awareness.

Much of the academic classroom program seems to have been conventional for its time, except for more individual attention to students; though my Unterterzia class had only six students, I also had individual tutoring in German and Latin throughout the year. All the Spetzgart students for this term are identified in the Archives, but there is no record, not even the names, of most of the teachers I remember. My nemesis among the latter was Herr Siegrest, who taught German and History and tutored me in Latin.

> *I don't like Herr Siegrest at all or Frau Schraube whom we have classes in Latin from (I have Latin from Herr Siegrest alone also). Thus I usually make fun of them in classes to everyone else's enjoyment as no one I know of likes Herr Siegrest.*

The only thing I'm going to claim to actually remember about Herr Siegrest's appearance is the scruffy black high shoes. Besides that I conjure a petulant if not irrascible old-fashioned bachelor, sallow complexion and grey-black cropped wiry hair, and a Pullman-green vest under an ill-fitting drab capelike long sweater. For the Pentecost holidays there was traditionally a four-day holiday when different teachers led tours of various kinds. This year it was postponed at the last moment by the Nazi authorities, but meantime I noted on June 11th that sign up sheets had been posted.

> *There is one big sailing tour under Herr Wutsdorft ... quite a few other juniors signed up but I don't think any of them have a chance. Herr Siegrest is also making one up but so far not a single person has joined up."*

Herr Siegrest was noted for administering *Ohrfeige*, a slap on the side of the head, and I received one of these in the second term, probably some time after the following entry:

> *Herr Siegrest has been getting worse and worse lately. When I first came here I pretended to be very innocent and he was one of the last to realize I wasn't and the things I said weren't just because I didn't know German.*

Later a slightly mellower note:

> *We found a mouse and put it in a cupboard. The next lesson was Deutsch by Herr Siegrest and we put it under a dish where he always sits down. He came in as usual and began yelling at everyone and then sat down at the table and as the dish was in the way of his books moved it away. The mouse jumped out and ran over his hand into the corner, and we all laughed so hard and paid so little attention to him that there was nothing left for him to do but to laugh too. Then we caught it again and put it under the dish, and the next lesson was English by a very dumb and fat lady. She got very scared and afterwards mad and yelled who had done this Frechheit and who was the Klassenordner.*

The last comment appears on November 10th, after we had been assembled for Hitler's radio talk:

> *Herr Siegrest gave us our first good German lesson by lecturing the whole time on the life of Hitler. I didn't understand much of this either but it seems the chief reason for Germany's losing the war was because of the Revolutionists and ammunition strikes at home.*

I wonder if Hahn might have been thinking of someone like Herr Siegrest when he said that he did not like school teachers, as in the following anecdote by Joseph Swire [4], which also illustrates his approach to recruiting staff. "An almost casual expression of interest in Gordonstoun methods brought from Hahn an invitation to stay with him ....Upon the third day of my visit he turned to me suddenly and said: 'You'd better join us.' I protested that I was no schoolmaster—I had instructed troops but never taught boys. 'That does not matter,' he replied, 'I do not like schoolmasters.' He explained that he wanted me chiefly to develop 'Projects.' 'But,' he went on to explain, 'we like each member of our staff to take part both in the practical and the academic sides. What could you teach?' I answered rashly that as I was a journalist I could perhaps manage English. 'But what about French? Surely, with your background, you could teach French.' To this I said that no, most emphatically I could not teach French, for I had lived in countries where French was a foreign language used only as ... ungrammatical jargon. Ultimately it was understood, at any rate by me, that I should have a very light timetable—a few periods of English ... but that the main purpose should be 'Projects.' My wife and I came to the school a week before the beginning of term. For my programme I was referred to the Chairman for modern languages. 'Your teaching timetable? Oh yes—here it is, all ready for you,' and he handed me a ruled blue card with every period filled. It was a full teaching programme. Every period was alloted to teaching French."

Every day I went to Frl. Ewald's quarters in the girls' wing for private tutoring in German with her mother. I found Frau Ewald more benign than Herr Siegrest. Two weeks after arrival:

> *In my German lessons with Frau Ewald I am reading a book which is a pretty exact copy of the American Tom Sawyer which of course I have read already. Thus it is easier but even then I can undersand it pretty well.*

A few days later:

> *I ate lunch with Frau Ewald on her porch as she has some boy to eat with her every lunch. The book I am reading now is called 'Tante Friede' and is very funny—I couldn't read* Tom Sawyer *very well and anyway Frau Ewald says that foreign books translated into German are usually rather badly written.*

The next to last entry about Frau Ewald records that I was learning my third poem, called the Heinzelmännchen, which was very long but not very hard.

Jocelin has recorded how he also was encouraged to memorize a German poem when he first arrived, eleven years old and not knowing a word of German [5]. Hahn did not care for prizes and seldom used them in his schools, but occasionally he would use a pedogogic wager to motivate a particular student. "A few days after arriving at Hohenfels I met Hahn on the stairway. 'How is it going?', in English naturally. I did not look very happy. 'What would you like best as a present?' I thought it over and said a hockey stick. 'Good; then I bet you that you can't memorize a German poem in the next week. If I lose, you get a hockey stick.' But Hahn had forgotten the wager when Jocelin recited a poem a few days later.

Some classes got better marks:

> Naturkunde *is lots of fun. We made experiments in dissolving salt and then letting it crystallize. This we did in two ways. One by heating it a great deal and the other by letting it stand eight days.The second way made the best crystals.*

Geography got fair marks. But Latin ran a close second to Herr Siegrest for disapproval. On July 10th:

> *We had a test in Latin in which I was a lot better although I still had only a five which is next to the worst,*

but the next day

> *I got a six again in the* Klassenarbeit. *Frau Schraube is sick so I don't have to go to her any more which is ein gluck. We had a Wettarbeit (a competition) in Latin with the other* Unterterzia *to see which was the best."*

> I was not so complacent about my poor showing in Math.

> *In the mathematics test I missed all the problems but only by a little which will probably make a better mark than missing half completely and having the others right—We had a mathematics* Klassenarbeit *in which I had to go out early and was thus not able to do the fourth and last problem which was very easy and I am sure I would have gotten correct if I had had the opportunity—We had another mathematics or algebra* Klassenarbeit *and I got four in it although one of the three problems we had Herr Fischer marked completely wrong was completely right so that ought to make my mark about two. Herr Fischer is now the best teacher we have in Spetzgart.*

The "now" refers to the fact that Herr Wutsdorf and Mr. Chew had departed after the first term.

Parents might gain some reassurance from the fact that despite my academic failure at Spetzgart, I later won one of the two National Scholarships to Harvard College awarded in California, which were based on a special seven-hour written examination. True, the subsequent career of the other winner may have discouraged the college from relying solely on examination results for admission; he got press notice during the war when he and some German POWs he was guarding down south surfaced on the wrong side of the Mexican border.

Service work has always been emphasized in the Salem schools, and the conception has changed with changing times. More recently it has been oriented towards ministering to the poor or elderly in nearby communities as well as to disaster relief in remote parts of the world. When I was at Spetzgart however, it consisted mostly of farm chores on the Markgraf's estates, which apparently provided a part of the school's meals. In late June:

> *I went over to some fields to put the hay that was in rows into stacks. First it has to be cut, then turned, then put in rows, then put in stacks and then the men come along with big wagons and collect it.*

It sounds as if these projects were preferable to Latin classes.

> *They dumped a huge load of coal in the front yard. The coal room is underneath and a tiny door is there for it to be shovelled through. It took about six boys all afternoon to get most of it down.*

In October:

> *I now have Waldarbeit. It consists of cutting down all the dead trees in a wood of small fir trees above Spetzgart and then rolling them down for firewood or to make steps out of. Being a new recruit I didn't get to cut down any trees and could only saw off the stumps which is a whole bunch of work.*

In November:

> *We had to dig up the dahlias which were very big and heavy and carry them up to the fruit room. It is in the basement and piled up to the ceiling with apples. At the end of it you come into another room full of jams and preserves and all kind of such things.*

Another day:

> *We were supposed to clean up the animal section. A lot of children have pets here but aside from two goats I don't think there is anything but rabbits. After that I had Strafarbeit all afternoon because of Frau Schraube's getting mad in Latin.*

In December:

> *In Waldarbeit we had to chop the ice off the path. It wasn't nearly as easy as it looked but Herr Fischer went away quite a lot and then we climbed down to the stream and tried to break through the ice.*

In the press Hahn's German and English schools are often called "elite," a word with some negative resonance. Some readers who know nothing else about the schools might be turned off by finding this word at the beginning of most popular articles. I probably would have been. It is a fact that the world of the local farmers was rather closed off from that of the school. But perhaps more relevant is the invariable diary designation of public school boys as "lausbuben." For example, regarding a train ride in the afternoon:

> *It isn't very good going third class because it is just at this time when all the* lausbuben *are coming home from their Volksschulen.*

The dictionary defines "lausbub" as "little rogue or rascal"; when we used the word the meaning may have been closer to what it sounds like in English.

Salem obviously originated in an aristocratic context, which may have reinforced some early elitist predilection in Hahn, and his emphasis on training for leadership. But I was unaware of any class distinctions *between* students at Spetzgart, and later equally unprepared to cope with them when I first did encounter them at Harvard college.The one exception at Spetzgart was a boy from Spain, who managed to make it clear to me that his "honour" was weightier than mine.

The archives record a Brahms Festival a week after my arrival. A regular Sunday morning music hour, piano and string instruments played by teachers and students, is duly noted. Alumni recollecting less politically disturbed periods often emphasize the important role of drama in school life, as in the memoir of Jocelin Winthrop-Young [7]: "Hahn believed in the theater as a means of education. At first Schiller and the Greek dramatists dominated but he soon began concentrating on Shakespeare, where the repeated failure of good and noble characters fascinated him and enabled him to show how they might yet have saved themselves. Acting gifts were of secondary importance. What he was looking for was strength of character, and bad behaviour would prevent inclusion. A well-known example is that of a boy who was to play Hamlet, but was caught out of bounds with a girl friend. After a long battle he was allowed to play Claudius! Hahn was holding to Plato, for clearly Plato had advocated that only people of good character should play good parts." In my year there were only several performances of plays and operettas written by students at Spetzgart. We did take the train over to Salem for the traditional Christmas play.

> *It was quite good. The devil who tells the king to kill all the babies was just about the best but the king himself wasn't bad and there were four shepards in it that all came from Spetzgart.*

Later, drama was ingeniously employed to keep the students quiet and busy during a scarlet fever epidemic, when we were required to memorize all of Schiller's "Wilhelm Tell" for a performance. The performance that impressed me most, however, was a game of charades that the girls played for us one evening after supper. The word to be guessed was "Bodensee."

> *The B was* Bauchweh, *the O was* Ohnmacht *or someone dying because they got a letter from their husband with bad news. D was a good one. Two of them as flappers sat down at the table and pretended to light cigarettes, and then the fat maid came in and said* 'Deutsche Frauen rauchen nicht' *(German women do not smoke).*

The craftwork program enlisted my interest more strongly than any school activity so far described. Prince Max's original conception of the role of craftwork depended on an earlier community of master artisans which was no doubt already in decline. In July 1919 he formulated it to

Hahn in this way [8]: "You want to start a public school here. Please remember you are on sacred Cistercian ground. The Cistercians owned this castle and this countryside from 1134 to 1803. They were the road-builders, the farmers, the foresters, the doctors, the consolers and the teachers of this district. The public school is only justified if it gives health to the district. To do this you must first receive health *from* the district. I do not want the craftsmen to come into this castle and teach in our atmosphere. I want you to send the boys to the craftsmen of the surrounding villages. You will find that the good artisan has a greater horror of half-finished work than the schoolmaster."

During my year there was one token compliance with Prince Max's request, when we went down to Überlingen to visit shops that worked with glass and made organs. I found it interesting to see how difficult it was to make organ pipes that had the correct tone. But by this time the shopwork was being done in the school buildings, and the blacksmith came up from Überlingen two afternoons a week on his motorcycle. The emphasis, at least for the younger students, was not on learning a craft but on somehow completing whatever object seized each boy's imagination, and when there were difficulties Herr Wenk often took the work back to his own shop. After a knife and a screwdriver, I started a copper bowl on a four-legged iron stand. The stand was already made, and the instructor did most of the forging of the bowl. It seemed to me that at least once during each shop period Herr Wenk had occasion to shake his head in resigned disapproval and remark that "they fought in the war" in response to some boy's chatter about the Jews. My major project was a safe box. Finished after many trials, the box prompted many ingenious speculations among my roommates about possible methods for breaking into it.

The two educational values that Hahn attached to craft work were seemingly incompatible: one to gain confidence from mastering things one was not naturally good at, and the other to discover a lifelong passionate hobby or career. There is a little of both, however, in the silversmith shop I have installed in my basement, fifty years after I was introduced to this craft by Herr Wenk. Both of the educational values are also documented in one of my favorite Hahn anecdotes, by Peter Saunders [4]:

"When I was about sixteen, Hahn sent for me and asked me what I was going to do with my life. I answered that very easily and clearly, as I had always been determined to become an actor, and said so. Hahn looked at me for a long time, with his penetrating blue eyes, whilst he picked up crumbs from the breakfast table with his right forefinger, and said, 'In your case my boy I must plead.' So I said, 'Plead what, Sir?' and he answered 'Plead with you not to do it.' 'Why,' I said, 'I think I would be rather good,' and he answered 'Yes, I think you would and it would ruin you.' So, a little facetiously I said 'Aren't you being slightly dramatic—surely it would not ruin me?' and he said 'Surely it would—you are vain and flamboyant, you would go to Hollywood and it would be the end of you.' I still did not take in what he really meant, so I said 'All right—what do you think I should do?' and without hesitation he answered 'You must take a piece of wood and saw through it carefully and well and when you hit a nail you must start again, without complaint—now you must leave me, as I am very busy.' In the best Gordonstoun tradition I went for a long walk and thought about what Hahn had said, and I realized there was much truth in it, whether I liked it or not. I had little humility, craftsmanship certainly bored me and I had no patience. From that moment on, I was determined to show Hahn that I could do better than he expected of me. When I came out of the Air Force aged twenty (I began) to painfully learn weaving, bought an old hand loom and set myself up in an attic in Aberdeen. Years later, when we were living a life of some comfort, surrounded by lovely things and a beautiful garden, I went for a walk with Hahn and said—'You see, obviously you were right and, let's face it, I did become a weaver.' To my astonishment he answered 'Yes, but a very flamboyant one'—and that was after twenty years."

Sailing had never engaged Hahn's attention, though it became one of his major enthusiasms later at Gordonstoun. It began at Spetzgart only after his departure, because of the school's location close to the shores of the Bodensee. The archives report [24] that in January 1933 the students began construction of a small harbour. The anonymous reporter rather laconically intermingled this and other events with Hahn's departure: "On March 11th Herr Hahn was taken into custody and had to leave the school. On the 16th he was released again. But so far forbidden to set foot in Baden. On the 17th we again got permission to build the harbour but 20 meters closer towards Sipplingen. The 21st was a school holiday to honor the reopening of the Reichstag (the Parliament building had burned three weeks before in a fire probably set by the Nazis). The Abitur exams began on the 20th at 3 PM and lasted until midnight. At 12:30 the Oberprima students learned they had all passed." I have included a photograph of some of these seniors, taken with their math teacher just after passing the Abitur.

In addition to some large conventional sailboats there were two undecked Cutters for the beginners, propelled either by ten oars or under sail after the two masts had been erected. My first outing on the lake, for which the boys dressed in blue pants and sweaters and white shirts, was on May 16th.

The hardest part of rowing in a big boat is to all row together. If your oar goes the littlest bit too deep or the littlest bit not deep enough it runs into one of the others. The captain of ours was Herr Wutsdorf or the man in charge of all the boating and afterwards he told Dennis I was good at it.

I was really hooked on the next outing a few weeks later.

Sunday afternoon I discovered just in time that some of the big boys including Jahn, the Guardian, were going out in a Cutter as there was a very good wind. They didn't want to take any more but luckily I got to go. It was marvelous. The wind was just right and we really went very fast. I didn't do much in the way of sailing it except for the jib. Every time Jahn swung the tiller around the boat would go way over on one side and the water almost came in several times. We tacked back and forth to get accross and then sailed back Beim Wind. It was the first time I have ever been sailing and I think it is piles of fun.

Later

I went sailing again so that made three days in succesion. I may get to be the main sail man as they have been letting me be it quite a lot, and I steered while they were changing tack. After supper Herr Wutsdorf gave a talk on his experiences as a submarine captain, and how he got the transport above Ireland. There were eighteen torpedo boats as guards on each side. At last he got off two torpedos though and one hit the engine and the other hit some other vital place so it sank. It was a big boat headed for America. Then a depth bomb from a British torpedo boat turned his submarine right over wrecking the electric motors so he had to come up in a hurry. It was night now and he was picked out of the water and taken prisoner.

The following Sunday after supper Herr Wutsdorf resumed his narrative with an account of his misadventures as a prisoner of war in England. All this was pretty stiff competition for Latin and Maths classes. By now he seemed to me to represent everything that was important about Spetzgart, even if his age and some eccentricities did not quite fit him for the role of youthful hero. If I had known that he would prove to be unsympathetic to the Salem schools, and one of the first to denounce Hahn to the Nazis, I would have been surprised but I'm afraid that my admiration would have been unruffled.

There are many further descriptions of sailing adventures, although I did not advance from the ten-oared Cutters to the Schwaben and the

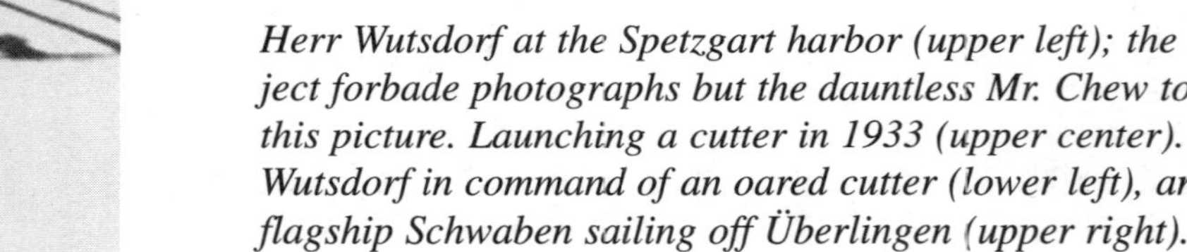

Herr Wutsdorf at the Spetzgart harbor (upper left); the subject forbade photographs but the dauntless Mr. Chew took this picture. Launching a cutter in 1933 (upper center). Herr Wutsdorf in command of an oared cutter (lower left), and the flagship Schwaben sailing off Überlingen (upper right).

Godenwind because the sailing program was a victim of the political storms in the following semesters. By far the longest entry in the Salem Diary describes a four-day tour around the lake during the second week in July, one of the Pfingsten tours that had been postponed. Jobst and I were among the ten boys who who took a Cutter with Herr Wutsdorf to Konstanz, out of the Bodensee proper, and then far down the Untersee where the Rhine finally flows out of the lakes, alternately rowing or sailing, except for the initial windless leg where we were towed by a motor boat in which Herr Wutsdorf had installed an old automobile engine. After the first night in a hotel on the Reichenau island, we sailed on stopping at Radolfzell and many other places to swim and fool around, and finally for the next night at what I described as a "peasant" school near Kattenhorn. Our hosts had boats with

> *peasant oars which don't require any turning as they are put on pegs,*

but this did not hinder them from beating us handilly in informal races that went on until after moonrise. We slept on the floor of the shop where they studied wood carving, on gunny sacks we had filled with hay from a hill behind the school. The fragrance of new mown hay was long remembered.

There were only a few occasions during this term when I was made aware of the conflicts that were developing between Salem and the Nazi regime, and which encompasssed also conflicts between different factions in the school staff and to some extent between different factions among Nazi functionaries. Two weeks into the term I noted:

> *Of course this school has a great pile of older boys that belong to the Hitler Jugend* [The Nazi youth organization for 14-18 year old boys]. *They have uniforms and march around on Saturday afternoon or sing songs. I think I forgot to write something that happened about a week ago. The head of all the schools in Baden, this county, who is known as the Prinz of Baden came and read something off a paper to us. He is very famous and he married I think the Princess of Norway or a Princess of Rumania. Another man who is a Prince of Rumania but was kicked out when he helped Germany in the World War was also there.*

The archives report [24] that Markgraf Berthold and Baron Hornstein came over from Salem to talk to a school assembly on May 22nd. They discussed an understanding with the leader of the Hitler Jugend in Baden that HJ uniforms could be worn at the school only on week ends, and that until further notice no student or teacher could be in illicit contact with Hahn. I compensated for not understanding the talk, at this early date, with a rather colorful identification of the speakers. The young Markgraf was actually married to a daughter of Prince Andrew of Greece, and a sister of the future Prince Phillip of England, who was to be a student at Spetzgart in the following term. I have always had an image of a visitor I thought to have been the Markgraf, in manner and appearance closely resembling Lech Walesa as he has appeared recently on television, but the photograph shows that this could not have been he. Perhaps the image, if not the Rumanian title, belonged to Baron Hornstein.

Some of the Hitler Jugend had regularly also been taking denunciations of staff members and school policies to the authorities in Karlsruhe (the provincial Capitol), as well as defiantly wearing the HJ uniform in place of the traditional school grey flannel. The Markgraf had obtained a compromise on the dispute about uniforms with a concession to Nazi demands that he prohibit staff and students from making contact with Hahn. The kind of contact that had infuriated the Nazis is suggested by a memorandum in the Salem archives [3]. A staff member had telephoned Hahn in Berlin, and asked how to deal with the HJ leaders. Hahn had passed meticulous judgment on the offending students in his old accustomed manner. The Nazi students were under no circumstances to be punished for their beliefs or their wish to wear their brown shirts at Salem; their offense was in using methods that had been declared improper not only by Salem, but also in the strongest terms by Reichsksanzler Hitler. The offense was more serious in the case of Hasenclever and Caesar (the leaders), because they were long-standing Nazis: both guilty of breaking their word. Two others should be judged more leniently, since they were still under the influence of earlier Communistic sentiments, to which they had been committed in *babyhafter* fashion.

The benevolent dismissal of teenage leftist radicalism as "infantile" strikes home; he would certainly have felt entitled to apply it to me a year after my leaving Spetzgart. The disparagement of my radical views would hardly have been acceptable to me then when I was fourteen, and sounds a bit unctuous even now. His use of the word *Babyhaft* does seem to express unequivocally his condescending attitude to Social Democrats of all ages and to the Weimar Republic. It could hardly have endeared him to to the Nazis that he condemned students for not obeying Reichskanzler Hitler, when only a few months before he had called on the alumni to "terminate their allegiance either to Hitler or to Salem." That Hahn could be persuaded to attempt such micromanagment by remote control seems fatuous in retrospect.

A laconic diary entry three weeks after the Markgraf's visit to Spetzgart momentarily opens a window onto much graver consequences of the waxing conflict with he Nazi authorities. On June 13th:

> *Tueday wasn't very eventful. In the morning we had a special school* Versammlung, *the purpose of which was the headmaster of the Schule Schloss Salem schools explaining a great many unpleasant things. In the first place (I couldn't understand very well and am not sure of everything) he said Fraulein Ewald was leaving request of the government (she was a Bolshevik or something); also that there wasn't nearly enough discipline here in Spetzgart and something about a new Kommissar. However despite all these terrible calamities the only really unpleasant thing he said was that there would be no tours. Wednesday morning was also not unusual only we had another school* Versammlung *in which the head man made more grave lectures and said how Herr Wutsdorf would now be the next highest person to him, and something about a big sport holiday.*

The canceled tours were the *Pfingsten* or Pentecost holiday trips; as already noted, I had been finagling two days earlier to be included in the group that would be sailing with Herr Wutsdorf. The four day cruise on the Bodensee finally took place in July, but only after the Nazi-inspired "sport holiday" had intervened.

Here are some reports from the school archives about the background of these events. On June 11th Frl. Ewald had announced [3] to a school assembly (which I evidently missed): "Most of you will already know from the newspapers that Herr Dr. Muller has been appointed Kommissar for the Salem schools (he had been director of the Oberreal school in Überlingen). He came to Salem this morning and informed us that he has instructions to conduct an investigation of Herr Dr. Meissner, Herr Mutscheller, Frl. Ewald, and Frl. Köppen (who was to be headmistress at Spetzgart during my next term). All these are furloughed until the investigation is finished. So tomorrow I will be on vacation. Herr Meese will be the academic director, although he probably still does not know it."

The speaker at the school assemblies noted in the diary was the newly appointed headmaster of Spetzgart, Dr. Meese, and his remarks are reported by several observers in the archives [3, 24]. "Hitler Jugend and Stahlhelm groups are suspended and are neither to appear in uniform nor to undertake anything else, such as for example was the case in the book burning [the infamous bonfires of May 10]. It is not that one does not wish them well, but only because there has been a great uproar over there [in Karlsruhe] as a result of the Hasenclever affair. The Ministry has informed me through the Kommissar that it puts great urgency on my taking control of both Instruction and Internat [other activities] until the matter of Frl. Ewald is decided. The Kommissar will come next week to inspect the whole school. For this reason we can not undertake the 4-day tours. We must now have only one concern, the survival of the principles of the school of Prince Max. You know me well enough not to take me for a drill-field type. I believe we will understand eachother. The Kommissar wants to protect the good reputation of Spetzgart. Any interferance by students ... immature youths.... After the uproar in Karlsruhe he has no sympathy for such high-handed behaviour of young people in opposition to their teachers."

Tuesday wasn't very eventful.

Aside from the cancellation of the sailing tour, this thirteen-year old was certainly not overly impressed by the announcement that our principal had been suspended by the Nazi Kommisar. Too bad they didn't get Herr Siegrest and Frau Schraube as well! My indifference disqualifies me as a critic of the awful silence of the German students at the time of Hahn's arrest. Still—there is a vast difference between a thirteen and an eighteen-year-old. Perhaps, if this had happened in the USA, there would have been a march on Überlingen, and a demonstration at the prison.

My indifference softened only a few days later when I went to the Ewalds' apartment for my usual German tutoring session.

> *In the morning I went as usual to the room of Frau Ewald and knocked at her door. After a while she came out and I could see she had been crying. She said she and her daughter had been asked to leave Germany (by the Nazis I suppose).*

I had grown fond of Frau Ewald. Though not recorded, I clearly remember what followed. The daughter, appearing impassively behind, took the mother by the arm, pulled her back into the room, and silently closed the door. I had had almost no contact with Frl. Ewald, so that this moment served to embody my impression of her as the best possible, i.e. the best that could be expected, of a woman principal. Someone firmly in charge but invisible, leaving important matters to Herr Wutsdorf and Mr. Chew, not messing about in the locker room or interfering in boys' personal affairs—in all these respects she was the antithesis of Frl. Köppen, who was to replace her in the next term.

The Kommissar had postponed the Pfingsten tours and now arranged that a festival, at first called an Olympiad, should intervene and introduce Spetzgart to the spirit of the new Germany. The archives report

[24] that on June 24th a Sonnenwandfeier (Midsummer festival) took place. "In the morning there was a field and track competition for the Juniors, and in the afternoon the seniors competed against the Stahlhelm and the Überlingen Turnverein. In the evening the whole school marched to Überlingen, where they joined a column that marched to a hillock near the town. There, according to ancient *germanic* custom, a *Scheiterhaufen* (a "funeral pyre"—the word also has some association with the medieval burning of heretics) was ignited.... Kommissar Muller gave a speech." The word "germanic" had not previously been featured in the school records, and foretold correctly that this was not to be an ordinary holiday:

> *Saturday was the day of the Olympiada. First there was the 100 meter which I wasn't very good in. In high jump I did 1 meter 17, the highest I ever was able to do before being l-10. In high jump Jocelin is marvellous. He did 1 meter 32 which is about on the level with his eyes, and was the best of the juniors with 63 points. Everyone who got over 40 points was supposed to get something. About half of the juniors got over 40, and I got 42.*

A page of diary records the complete scores for twenty one boys. All the over 40s are underlined; Nickolaier got 35, and Jobst got 15—this score is underlined, and then the line is crossed out, I think not through error but to call attention to the disgraceful performance. After some disparaging comments on the seniors' afternoon track meet and soccer game, the account continues:

> *After supper I piled into a big bus with about fifty others although I didn't know where I was going or what for. We drove down to the Überlingen soccer platz where gradually troops and troops of Hitlerites and citizens began to arrive. There were two bands and the soldiers marched around some, and then the whole kaboodle started off—there must have been around a kilometer of people. It seems as if the Germans are never happy unless they are marching. We left the road later on and after wading through mud for a long way reached the destination. It was a hilltop commanding a marvelous view and really a more picturesque thing I have never seen. Two solitary tall trees were illuminated when the fire was started. From all the surrounding hilltops you could see fires burning despite the slight rain. The fire was a giant affair that sent up great clouds of flame. Several people got their clothes caught on fire by the sparks. They sang some songs about the flame of the men's hearts who died in the World War for Germany and everyone seemed to be*

A group of Spetzgart seniors who graduated in the spring of 1933, shown with their math teacher just after passing the Abitur exam (upper left). Seated fifth from the left is Uli von Oertzen, who perished in the nearly successful attempt to assassinate Hitler on 20th July 1944. The author typing his diary (upper right); Erwin Strauss took this picture as the sun set over the Bodensee, and made the original postage stamp sized print himself. Below: Jobst Frowein, and the legendary high jump event at Spetzgart in 1934: staff and students have gathered en masse to applaud progress by the least gifted as well as by the champions.

very much for Hitler. Things like that can't be put onto paper. They just won't fit into a flat piece of black and white.

My eloquence faltered when I was deeply impressed, but I hardly doubt I would have been eager to join the Hitler Jung Volk after this Midsumnmer festival. More eager than Jobst was, who would resignedly say *"Dass muss man machen jetzt"* [you have to do that now] during the next term. If it had been only a school festival it would not have had the same impact. But here I was marching through the night in a vast column of grownup men in uniform, and seeing then in the distance the great bonfires of similar groups on every hilltop as far as the eye could see. It seems inconceivable that I could have been an enthusiast a year later, but then there never was a year later, because at fourteen back in California I came under the influence of Phillip MacDougal. Phillip was the only boy my age within walking distance of home, and when I went away his highest aspiration had been shooting ground squirrels with his grandfather. Now all was changed. He was a Communist (a little less *babyhaft* than I), reading *Erewhon* and *South Wind*, and a follower of the spiritual leader Krishnamurti. We spent afternoons in a converted toolshed, drinking tea and listening to classical records, *Das Kapital* unread on a shelf overhead while we applauded the San Francisco General Strike.

For a long time after this I harbored a vague notion that the problem with the Germans must be that their development was always arrested at age thirteen. But in a recent book, *Inside Nazi Germany,* on everyday life Detlev Peukert has documented that "durable loyalty could not be generated by [such] solstice ceremonies alone," the Volksgemeinschaft united around hilltop bonfires while cowering in the darkened valleys below were Jews, gypsies, homosexuals, the mentally ill, and long-haired layabouts. Disenchantment was in fact relatively conspicuous among 14- to 18-year-old boys in Germany. Mass rituals of this kind were "capable of generating manic and intoxicated moods for shorter and shorter periods," and after 1935 were mostly discarded as the vacuity of the vague goal of building a "national community" by such means became apparent to young and old alike.

CHAPTER 5

A School in Conflict with the Nazis

The conflict in the Salem Schools during the first six months of the Nazi regime involved not only the personal jeopardy of the founder and of the staff members who were seen as sympathetic to him and his principles, but also the continued independent existence of the schools. If only fragments of these long past events can be remembered I want to describe them, as far as possible, using authentic voices of some of the participants and observers.

When I wrote to the school to ask if I might visit and explore the records, a welcoming reply came from my English schoolmate of sixty years ago, Jocelin Winthrop-Young. He had been Headmaster at Salem for a year in 1963, and among other roles had since organized the archives, of which his daughter, Sophie Weidlich, was the current curator.

When he left Spetzgart at the end of my first term, Jocelin had been the first student to enroll In Hahn's new school in Scotland, and after graduation had served as a British naval officer in the Pacific during the war. Then in 1949 the King of Greece had approached Hahn to found a school there in which he could enroll his son, Prince Constantine. In one of his famously persuasive telephone calls, Hahn had enlisted Jocelin, who served as director of the Anavryta school for a decade, until the changing political tides made a British teacher unwelcome in Greece. I suspect that, while anxious to recruit him for the cause, Hahn may have felt comfortable keeping him somewhat removed. Jocelin returned to Salem and had stayed on as advisor to the board, and director of an affiliated conference of schools around the world whose philosophy and ideals were inspired by Hahn's example. In 1994 this "Round Square" Conference included eleven schools in Europe, five in North America, two in Australia, four in India and one in Kenya.

After an early summer tour of Provence with our bicycle club in 1991, Tomoko and I took the train from Avignon to Konstanz and, our bicycles having arrived at the station the next morning, loaded the panniers and under blue skies on this balmy day took the ferry across the Bodensee to Meersburg. After lunch on a waterfront terrace we followed quiet back roads up through forested hilltops and down again to the cultivated level cropland of the intimate Salem valley. Villages every three or four miles where they had always been but I noted clusters of seemingly new two or three story apartments or townhouses. In between them, wheat fields or orchards reaching to the very edge of every road and village, uninterrupted by minimalls, housing tracts, billboards, discount or franchised emporia.

A second floor corner room was reserved for us at the Gasthof Schwanen, a mile from the village and just outside the lower Gate House of the Markgraf's compound. Soon after our arrival a handwritten notice appeared on the bulletin board downstairs: *"Wilkommen Familie Flavin"* The Schwanen retains souvenirs of 1684 when it was built as guest house for the Cistercian monastery. An oven still breaks through the wall of each room so that fuel can be added from the hallway, and I especially admired the simple wrought iron fixtures made in the blacksmith shop inside the compound which, however, is no longer available for student use.

This afternoon after settling into the Schwanen we wandered under the Gate House and into the vast grassy court enclosed by castle, cathedral and *langbau* (monastic building). Giant copper beach trees, a statue commemorating an ancestor from the Franco-Prussian war, an odd steep cobbled walkway down to the vigorous steam running under the grounds, designed for bathing horses. An elegantly dressed crowd was gathering in the distance on foot, though a few black Mercedes and BMWs had also penetrated into the court through other gates. It was Commencement day. One travels by bicycle at the expense of being well dressed. We beat a retreat.

Jocelin and his German wife Sybylle introduced themselves while we were having dinner that evening in the patio, where they could spot us from their gatehouse apartment. The next morning and for a week, while Tomoko bicycled around the valley, I visited the archives in a room off the hallway of the floor they occupied in the ancient gate house.

As we know, Hahn had been arrested and imprisoned at Überlingen on March 11th 1933 (arbitrary arrest in the name of "protective custody" had been authorized by decree on February 28th, the day after the Reichstag fire). On March 16 he was released but banned from the province of Baden, and in July he escaped to England, where in the following November he founded a school in Scotland on Salem principles.

While it might have seemed that "escape" overdramatized his departure, it is quite possible that without the intervention of influential supporters he could have been in mortal danger. Indeed the month of his departure saw the opening of the first concentration camp at Dachau, near Munich; a month later it already contained thousands of poltical prisoners and some were already being brutally murdered there at this time. A Catholic editor who had also criticized Hitler's response to the Potempa murders, Fritz Gerlich, was shot at Dachau in the purge of 1934. There is also an unconfirmed story [9] that shortly before his arrest Hahn had planned to accompany a school team that was competing in Switzerland, and was prevented by a friendly constable who had learned of a plan by local Nazis to stop him at the border and shoot him for attempting to escape abroad.

Intervention at the highest level was due to the efforts of Sir Neville Butler, whom Hahn had befriended in Berlin when, as an English student, he had been interned at the onset of World War I. Butler describes [4] how this came about: "In March 1933, as his secretary, I was with the Prime Minister and Ishbel MacDonald at the Beau-Rivage Hotel in Geneva. At dinner, a lady at a nearby table caught my eye, and presently a waiter brought me a note. She was Mrs. Arnold-Forster and had just come from Salem School where she had been teaching. The note told me that the Nazis had put Kurt in prison and that I 'must get him out.' I knew that it would be diffcult for my Chief to intervene as he had, on principle, declined to do so on behalf of various old Social Democratic leaders whom the Nazis had persecuted." The secretary drafted a letter for the Prime Minister, with the following note [3]: "In 1914-15 I owed Hahn almost everything—except money. If the Nazis do persecute him (as a hated Jew)—and he has been under arrest a week, his numerous friends mean to start a press agitation—which will not help." On 17 March Ramsay MacDonald wrote [3] the German Foreign Minister von Neurath: "Please take this as a purely personal letter ... Hahn is a familiar figure in Oxford ... and has worked hard to create friendships between our two countries.... He has spent many summers in a certain neighbourhood in my native Morayshire, which is particularly dear to me and children of several of my friends have been at his school. If your are able to take a friendly interest I believe it will be a service to both our countries." A perfunctory reply from von Neurath alleged that he had already intervened and caused Hahn to be released before receiving the Prime Minister's letter.

The young Markgraf Berthold addressed the following letter [9] to

Hitler himself a week before the Easter vacation: "In 1919 my father donated the Schule Schloss Salem to the German people. I am prepared to renew this gift. I can do so because for thirteen years I have promoted in every fundamental respect, by education for honesty and courage, the goals you have established for the development of character in the German people in your book Der Kampf.... But today I am threatened with having to close the school. The cofounder Hahn has been arrested, and then exiled from Baden.... Until now his banishment has not been lifted. This situation has spread distrust and dismay in the parents. The withdrawals increase, the anxious enquiries are ceaseless, and new applications are not forthcoming. I can not control this panic until the original blunder of the arrest is corrected, i.e. until the return of Hahn to Baden and Salem is authorized. To this end I beg for an order from the Herrn Reichskanzler that will protect the school from further suspicion. But if, Herr Reichskanzler, you can not trust us, I would be grateful for a candid statement, and I am prepared to take the responsibility to terminate the Salem enterprise." Absent an answer, the Markgraf is said to have tried to call on Hitler in person, who screamed at him in public: "Why don't you aristocrats get rid of your *Hofjuden* [Court Jews]?"

Rudolf Hess in particular was repeatedly asked to intercede, and is believed ultimately responsible for instructions that the school be preserved. Thanks to English friends, Hahn's sister in law Lola was able to see him, a few hours before Hitler was scheduled to visit. Kuchenmüller, the ardent Nazi teacher at Salem who was expelled from the party for his defence of Hahn, also described visiting Hess in a memorandum written fifty years later[14]: "He listened to me attentively as I told him of Hahn's meritorius posture during the Versailles period. He promised to do his best for Hahn. That a jew could continue to be a teacher of German youth seemed most unlikely. Whether it stemmed from his influence I do not know. Hahn was released, but was allowed his freedom only outside of Baden....Gauleiter Robert Wagner had insisted on this exile.... Hopefully my readers know that later Rudolf Hess suffered a much harder portion than Hahn; he remains guiltless in prison, now for more than three decades."

Ten years earlier Kuchenmüller and Hahn had been adversaries in a debate on anti-semitism at Salem. In 1923 Golo Mann had prepared a critical report of Hitler's Munich beerhall putsch for the school newspaper, which appeared monthly in two handwritten copies [13]. Frl. Ewald had asked him to withdraw it in favor of a debate: "This sort of one-sided report could sow dissension," she told him, "[since] within the Salem community there was a wide range of political opinions, even among the pupils, but more so among the teachers." Mann described the debate, which took place at a school assembly. Kuchenmüller opened with a poem beginning "I am born to feel a German..," then quoted some unpleasant lines by a Jewish poet. A young math teacher, more fanatical than Kuchenmüller, described how the German Jews in uniform had usually held desk jobs.

Mann himself found his written eloquence faltering in public debate. But the Guardian Prince Berthold hit the nail on the head: he did not see how one could judge people by their race or religion. Hahn, who this time had not wanted to preside, spoke next to last, refuting the assertion that German Jews had been bad soldiers, to which Kuchenmüller replied that we should not believe every thing that Herr Hahn, of all people, had to say—an allusion to the Headmaster's Jewishness. Noisy and angry protest came from all present.

"In reality many things fit together that the books will tell us are irreconcilable," Mann adds as a postcript. After his expulsion from the party in 1933, Kuchenmüller headed a country boarding school in the forest where he protected young Jews as long as he could.

That the arrest and banishment of Hahn was not sufficient to ensure the school's survival is clear from an article of June 3 1933 that appeared in the *Bodensee Rundschau* under the heading: "On the Schloss Schule Salem: Sinister Operations of the Jew Hahn:"

"It is vitally important that certain events in the Salem schools be more widely publicized. The students are drawn from feudalistic, and particularly from wealthy Jewish capitalist circles. At this time there are 20 to 30 Jewish students. The inmates are hermetically sealed off from the outside world (for example they wear special uniforms). Herr Hahn saw his principle mission to be to raise these students on Jewish-pacifist principles. He recruited a teaching staff that was completely in sympathy with his goals.

"Clearly the National Socialist Revolution could not stand by indifferent to this state of affairs. Hahn had to be removed. The direction was taken over by the Markgraf Berthold von Baden, who however openly continues under the influence of Hahn. The staff shows a suspicious zeal to put on the air of sturdy patriots and to parade their connections with the leaders of the New Germany like Alfred Rosenberg, Hess and Buttmann. They seem to confuse the National Socialist Germany with the old system which always capitulated to people with grand connections.

"After his release from custody, Herr Hahn is busy again exercising his baleful influence over the Schloss Schule. By reckless chicanery he had during his tenure prevented students, who despite all discouragements were seized by the idealistic vitality of the young Germany, from joining the National Socialist youth organization. This corrupter of youth stopped at nothing. Students were taken at night by car to a forest near Sigmarinen, where Hahn belabored them under no conditions to join the Hitler Jugend. Attempts were made to incite parents through circular letters. All this could take place under the direction of the Markgraf!

"When these things became known in Karlsruhe, three teachers were dispatched here who tried by all kinds of tricks to prevent the formation of a Hitler Jugend group. At the same time these gentlemen, one of whom bore a noble name and a Stahlhelm insignia, had the incredible impudence to babble something to the students about personal conflicts between Adolf Hitler, Dr. Göebbels and Göering.

"Much remains to be done. The Jewess Richter and other teachers are still in place, whose hostility to the National Socialist Revolution is well known. These people are still seeking the return of the Jew Hahn, and there is grounds for suspicion that they are still consulting with Hahn."

The *Rundschau* article here puts the responsibility for the Nazis' disapproval of Jewish teachers entirely on the Jews themselves, and their hostility to the regime, a truly extraordinary idea that seems never to have completely vanished in Germany. Sixty years later a German professional historian, Ernst Nolte, is apparently proposing again that the Jews in some ways actually provoked the holocaust; a view that is, to be sure, stirring widespread disapproval among his academic colleagues. The *Runschau* article concludes:

"The Salem school must therefore continue to be kept under close observation. The best final solution would be for a Kommissar to be installed, which seems the only appropriate measure, and for the school to be merged with the other Baden schools."

The lull before the storm continued for two months after Hahn's arrest [26]: "At first it looked as if the school itself would not be attacked. Under Herr Baumann and Herr Mutscheler [at Salem] the term proceeded in an orderly fashion to the end. But after the easter vacation the battle began. Complaints against the school and against individual staff piled up threateningly; denunciations from within our own ranks unfortunately also played an ominous role." The principal roles in the conflict that followed were of course played by staff at the parent school, people who I had never met. The following account highlights the roles played by students and staff at Spetzgart, whom we have already encountered in Chapter 4.

I could not see the written denunciations kept in a locked file in the school archives, but I was told that among Spetzgart staff who had denounced Hahn were Herr Wutsdorf and Herr Schraube (the husband of my Latin tutor). Wutsdorf and others had gone to Berlin soon after Hahn's arrest to protect themselves; there is a record of a phone call Wutsdorf made from Berlin to Frl. Rokol, saying he would be loyal to Salem, but he was not.

The open record has a bit more about student denunciations of staff members, paricularly about two seniors at Salem who were organizing a Hitler Jugend group. At Spetzgart there was "feverish stitching of brownshirts for the Hitler Jugend, which has appeared in uniform since May 1st. There are twenty of them [27]" On May 16th Herr Meissner reports his phone call on behalf of the staff at Salem to the Minister of Culture at Karlsruhe [3]: "The Ministry called my attention first to today's letter directing that Caesar should organize a Hitler Jugend group. My answer was that Herrn Baumann and Kuchenmüller would be presenting a petition there today. It was our opinion that the Ministry must be inadequately informed about our attitude. The Ministry answered that the gentlemen from Salem had been explicitly informed by the appropriate authorities today, and closed the conversation with an emphatic warning: 'Be very circumspect in the way you handle this matter. We will not tolerate any sabotage of the Hitler Jugend in Salem, regardless of who should attempt it.'"

The next day there was a letter from Karlsruhe to Unterprima student Caesar [3]: "Comrades! You have complete freedom of action. Get on with your work at once. The gentlemen were here and after I ascertained that they wanted to hinder you I did not need to negotiate further. We phoned the school director and told him point blank that we would under no circumstances tolerate any interferance with the young revolutionaries of the Hitler Jugend."

Three weeks later a diary [28] reports a joint Salem-Spetzgart colourbearers meeting on June 10th about another Salem senior: "Promises not kept. Denunciations. Hasenclever denies, then gives his explanation. Requests for his clarification of the attack in a newspaper article. Sly stories which he took to Karlsruhe about a history class of Herr Meissner's. Hasenclever loses the colours." On the following day three separate contingents set out for the Ministry : "Hans Jung, (the Guardian at Spetzgart), and other colourbearers go very early to Karlsruhe. Separately Herrn Baumann and Deubner. Behind them Hasenclever and Caesar."

But by now Herr Meissner had been dismissed. A Kommissar had been appointed, from the local Oberrealschule in Überlingen, to take complete charge of the schools. On June 13: "Jungstahlhelm and Hitler Jugend are dissolved until further notice by Kommissar Muller. Herr Muller thanked Hasenclever for his commendable work in the Hitler Jugend, and elicited a three-fold 'Sieg Heil.'" Herr Meissner subsequently followed a path of resolute defiance of the Nazi regime. Reinstated for a time, he narrowly escaped from Germany in 1934 to join Hahn at Gordonstoun school.

The installation of a Kommissar, a week after it had been recomended in the Rundschau editorial, must have been the eventuality most dreaded up to now by those faithful to Salem traditions. A diary records [26]: "'Downfall' is said to have been shouted again at a staff meeting at the Gasthof Schwanen." Although Kommissar Muller's first move was to temporarilly suspend the Hitler Jugend, he lost no time in confirming the expectation that this intervention threatened the school with imminent *Gleichschaltung* or submersion in Nazi ideology. Already in 1933 the leader of the Nazi Teacher's League and Bavarian Minister of Culture Hans Schemm had lectured Professors at the University of Munich [29]: "From now on it is not up to you to decide whether or not something is true but whether it is in the interests of the National Socialist Revolution."

Fräulein Ewald, headmistress at Spetzgart, has left a long and systematically prepared record [30] of her encounters with the Kommissar during the six weeks of his tenure. But first some excerpts from two more spontaneous diaries [27,28] may give a better sense of what this period felt like to staff and older students. "June 12. Cat injured by a thrown stone. During the night shots fired from the west or southwest wing. Why knows anything? No one. But many chimed in on the question of who has a pistol etc. Deposit them in the firearms cabinet; not to spread disorder ... June 13. Herrn Muller and Grüninger (Nazi youth leader from Konstanz) make their headquarters in the business office of Baron Hornstein. Here is the main telephone. Baron Hornstein's secretary sits in the outer room ... June 19. Frl. Ewald has now been furloughed for a week. There are depositions under oath. Denunciations ... June 27. The Kommissar here for hours. Only selected people met with him. Frl. Ewald sits up in her house, works in the garden, but is not with us. Several people try to convince the Kommissar that he should not listen exclusively to people with antipathies. There is a bad atmosphere here. Two parties stand against each other, and the little circle around the new dictator is very busy ... June 29: Frl. Rokol also denounced and then put under house arrest, but after an explosive discussion from almost all the staff the Director of Studies agreed to intercede. The whole school is now upside down. One catastrophe after another. All authority for girls has gone over to the Schwester. For days the whole buildng has been pitch dark in the evenings. Electric failure. This did enable unspied-on meetings in the evenings. One could hazard this even if under house arrest. In these days crows fluttered about the buildings ... July 9. Yesterday news spread through the school like a forest fire. Spetzgart will be closed. Decision tomorrow. Student opposition to some teachers in the classroom is no longer inhibited ... July 12. Staff assembly under Director of Studies Meese. From now on no criticism is allowed of persons charged with the direction. Anyone violating this would be discharged without notice. Fürst Sturdza responded with a princely bomb: under these conditions he would resign. Mr. Chew, the Englishman, seconded him. The shocked Director of Studies: 'that's impossible, you have your contracts.' There was even a shout from in back: 'They're both drunk.' The Guardian was heard to say 'Everyone who doesn't knuckle under will now fly away.'"

From Chapter 2 we see that not much of this registered with a junior student at Spetzgart, but I have one memory brought back by the mention of gunfire at the beginning. One night my roommates and I were wakened by some disturbance outdoors. In a fourth floor room accross the hall we found Mr. Chew and a young woman teacher peering out into the darkness below through an open window. Mr. Chew was not wearing the bottom half of his pajamas. His *sang-froid* under these circumstances was awesome to me. And I don't doubt that, if Hahn had been present, the conviction he brought back to Berlin during the first war that England could never be defeated would have been fortified.

Fraulein Ewald wrote a long personal account [30] of the first three weeks after the installation of the Kommissar, revealing the Nazi procedure for taking control of a school. On June 11 Frl. Köppen came to Spetzgart to notify her that Dr. Meissner had been furloughed, and she at once sought out the Guardian Hans Jung who called a Helper Assembly. "Frl. Köppen repeated that she was acting as a messenger only because of her car, and did not want the students to hold it against her. I observed how awkward it was that I had learned about it in this way." The staff had learned of the Kommisssar's appointment only from the newspapers. "The Helpers reported that they were prepared to go to Karlsruhe and in the evening went to Salem for a joint Helper conference. Frl. Köppen and I went to Herr Meese (hitherto Director of Studies and accordingly subordinate to Frl. Ewald) and asked him if he was prepared to stick up for Dr. Meissner. He deplored the 'great number of calamities' that had befallen the school, such as the circular letter to the parents, and was indignant that his advice had not been solicited." June 12. "Learned from

Dr. Meissner that the Kommissar would also be obliged to ask Frl. Köppen, Herr Mutscheller and myself to accept furloughs." June 13. "Dir. Meese informed me in writing that until things were finally settled Herrn Wutsdorff would take charge. Frl. Rokol and Mr. Chew informed Herrn Dir. Meese that they could not accept Herrn Wutsdorf." June 22. "It occurs to me that probably no one has spoken in support of me, as Dr. Meese often sees the Komissar. I deliberate whether to ask Oberforstrat Meiss, as a father and longstanding neighbour, to go to the Kommissar." Later "I went to see the Oberforstrat and told him that in my opinion the interrogation could not possibly reveal anything and asked if he could perhaps make enquiries."

June 24. "Midsummner day. At Spetzgart I watched the children's track meet, before a noon appointment with the Markgraf. The Markgraf told me I was accused of having said that Hitler was a murderer. He had immediately challenged that as impossible. I told him about the incident when in the presence of Herrn v. Hornstein Herrn Wutsdorf had made this accusation against me in a great rage, after we had told him we thought it would be unsuitable for us to work together with him any longer. I had replied then: 'But Herrn Wutsdorf, if you really believed you heard me say something which you well knew in no way corresponded to my convictions, surely you would have said: did I hear correctly?' Whereupon Herr W. retracted, and said he had been told I said it. Then he explained he would resign soon, to go back and look after the welfare of the sister and her children."

June 26. "Monday morning I went to see the Kommissar. He spoke much of the difficulty of his position, and how much easier I would make it for him if I would request the furlough, and at the same time try to present this step to parents and children in a positive light. We spoke of a temporary transfer to Hohenfels." June 27. "The Kommissar came to Spetzgart with Herrn Grüninger and was received by Herrn. Wutsdorf. Other adults who were anxious to see him told me that they were not admitted since he had met only with Herrn. W. and Director Meese, and had accepted a phone call from Frau Schraube. At noon I was summoned to the Kommissar, who asked me in the presence of Herrn Grüninger about my decision. I spoke of a transfer to Salem. The Kommissar said this was out of he question, as was any other continuation, as on top of the accusation about calling Hitler a murderer two more had been added: first, that I had said that the new regime would mean the end of culture, one need only look at the faces of the leaders, G and G looked like butchers; and second, a story about an imitation of Hitler's deranged voice by an alumnus, which had made me laugh so hard I fell under the table. The

Kommissar would not identify the denouncers or allow me to confront them. That would involve an adversarial proceeding that was beyond his jurisdiction."

June 28. "Frl. Rokol called, very upset and in tears. The Schwester had accused her to Dr. Meese of having referred to my 'denunciation.' Dr. Meese had at once reported this to the Kommissar and she, Rokol, would now also be furloughed." Her offense was the use of the word "denunciation." Under the "Malicious Practices Act" of 21 March 1933 citizens had been charged with reporting to authorities any remarks insulting to the Reich or degrading to the national revolution. But the Nazis were sensitive to the word "denunciation," which they liked to associate with bolshevik abuses. Our own shame need not be enhanced, if it could be, by this counterfeit sensistivity, for the record of anonymous denunciations that were solicted during the McCarthy period, when some of the best American universities fired teachers for refusing to denounce others.

Later on June 28 Fr. Ewald had her final meeting with the Kommissar at Salem. "The Kommissar dictated to Herr Grüninger a series of vile and unbelievable reproaches against me: I was even now influencing the children in crafty ways, I had created an uproar at Salem by my visit yesterday, one could attach too much importance to my indispensability and I was not in a position to seek the halo of a martyr. I said that if there had been an uproar at Salem, it could only have resulted from the news of the prolongation of my furlough. The Kommissar replied that the impact of my furlough could be easily ascertained. One would simply gather all the boys and girls together in Spetzgart and say: 'Those who want to stay with Frl. Ewald, go to one side, those who want to stay here to the other.' In conclusion he asked me whether I would not now make an end of all this by leaving Spetzgart; I had also dragged Frl. Rokol into it, who would have a by no means pleasant quarter hour with him tomorrow and would presumably also be furloughed. I seemed to have misused the word 'denunciation.' So far the proceedings had been on a gentlmanly basis, he hoped they would not be propelled in a direction which would force the Ministry to resort to other measures. He asked if I had any other financial stake in the school. I said that the yacht 'Schwaben' belonged to me, and I held a mortgage on the branch at Hermannsberg. He said that Frl.Köppen and I also had life insurance policies, the amounts of which he also specified. At the end he was again polite and took his departure with a handshake, which greatly astonished me." June 29. "The Markgraf called to tell me that he had been forced to add the words 'for a year' to my request for a furlough."

Herr Wutsdorf, my idol at Spetzgart, former submarine commander and admiral of the Bodensee fleet, emerges from this sadly tarnished. His story has not been preserved in the school archives, so finally he too is not allowed to confront his denouncer.

Reading Frl. Ewald's account today, it seems hard to escape thinking that she probably did say all the things which she was accused of saying by the Kommissar, and to wonder why she denied the accusations so categorically. She did not need the job to survive, like many teachers in those days of thirty per cent unemployment. She had known Hahn ever since schoolgirl days. He would have exhorted her to stay at her post and save the school at any cost, and it was undoubtedly her loyalty to him which she would not compromise and which the Nazis could not tolerate. When even the posession of a photograph of Hahn jeopardized a career she went to see him in prison, and later until the war visited him periodically in Scotland. Other things were also at stake. It was only four years since she had been appointed head of the new branch at Spetzgart, in an experiment which was to determine whether the principles of Hahn could survive in a secondary school without his physical presence, and under the guidance of a woman at that.

A memoir written fifteen years later [24] notes of this period that "Kommissar Muller, who had at first adopted a severe approach and was obviously prejudiced against Salem in his investigation, found that he was unable after several weeks stay to prove any politically subversive activity. He reported the result of his investigation to the Ministry and at the same time supported the continued existence of the school. Direktor Muller had recognized something of value in Salem during his interrogation of individual students, especially the Helpers. The regime wanted now to make use of this for National Socialism, by coordinating us with them and eliminating opposition (Gleichschaltung)." We have seen that during this time the student Colourbearers and Helpers had been calling their own assemblies and sending delegations to the provincial capitol to defend the school, entirely independantly of the staff. These student leaders, "prefects with ministerial portfolio" in Jocelin Winthrop-Young's phrase, were vindicating Hahn's delegation of vital responsibilities in a way that impressed even the Kommissar.

An extraordinary reversal now occured [26]. In accord with the threat which closed the Markgraf's letter to Hitler "The school asociation now seriously considered whether they should take it upon themselves to close down the school, as it appeared it would be compelled to assume a different character. But now it was revealed that decisions were no longer our prerogative. Ministerialrat Kraft, who came as a representative of the

Ministry to reorganize Salem, was so enraged by the idea that the Association might choose to close the school that he exacted a continuation by means of the most severe threats in a memorable meeting with the Markgraf." The threats on this occasion evidently included arrest and imprisonment.

At some higher level in the Party it had been decided to preserve Salem, overriding the hostility of local members expressed in the Bodensee Rundschau articles. Why? Probably, for two reasons. The realization that it could be a good source of army officers, which played a greater role later during the war years, is illustrated by excerpts from a letter at this time [31] from General von Brauchitsch to Hitler: "I am asking if your honour might take an interest in the preservation of the four schools comprising the Salem school establishment in Baden. I know the school at first hand. In 1931 I enrolled my second son because I was convinced that he would be educated there according to my principles of patriotism and character development, would learn to serve and to lead, and be prepared for a military career." Later the letter touches on the second reason for preserving Salem: "The school has maintained excellent relations with leading public figures in England, as a consequence of which they have sent their sons to Salem. It seems certain that the English would not send their children to a German state school if it became officially committed to National Socialist training, and this were outwardly expressed by its being placed under the direction of a government Kommissar and by obligatory wearing of the brown uniform."

Three months later a letter [32] from Ministerialrat Kraft himself to a former teacher from England (Ka Arnold-Forster) confirms, while touching on other things, the concern that the regime had at this time to maintain good relations with England. "In your letter you ask if the 'spying systerm, which was officially sanctioned in Salem recently,' has now been definitively set aside ... I have seen nothing of it. I also can not imagine that it was in any way promoted from our side, since such bolshevik methods are not in our line. We could not blame the children if they were indignant about derogatory remarks about great men of German history by teachers with a Marxist orientation. English students would also not have been pleased by such false statements about their country and history. But the days when such remarks could go unpunished in Germany are finally passed.... In answer to your second question, Frl. Ewald is still furloughed—her remarks about the present Reichskanzler were so offensive that at least half a year must pass before this impudence can be forgotten.... Unfortunately I must inform you that Mr. Young has not brought his son back to Salem, although he had formerly promised me he would do so. I would be grateful if you could inform me why this has not taken place."

It was in order to serve as a bridge to England, and hopefully to some of its leading public figures, that Salem was allowed to survive without completely adopting the Nazi educational program. More than any other aspect of Nazi foreign policy the persistent, hopeless goal of an alliance with England was hatched directly trom the mind of Hitler himself. The daydream was of a European continent under Germany while the nearest cousins to the master race continued to administer their colonies around the world. The first major initiative, a bilateral naval treaty with Britain in 1935, proved also to be the last; the military and industrial leaders backing Hitler gave no support. The dream survived until and even after the two countries were at war, as documented by the Nazi plot to sequester a potential Quisling by kidnapping the Duke of Windsor from Lisbon in June 1940, and finally perished only a year later with Hess's unauthorized parachute landing at the estate of a Scottish duke. In a teacher's report [33] of the endless problems at Salem in 1934-36, which tries to close optimismtically by noting that "Salem enjoys the greatest prestige in foreign countries," there is an uncaptioned photograph of the Duke of Windsor chatting with a senior student.

Having forced the continued existence of the school, against its own wishes, Ministerialrat Kraft addressed an assembly at Salem at the end of my first term [34] to set forth some principles by which it was henceforth to be guided and to introduce the new Director chosen by the regime:

"Dear students,

"It is now about two months since I last visited here in this room and in this short interval the world-shaking events in Germany have by and large achieved their fulfillment. As I told you then, I had the impression that the waves of these events had not billowed uncurtailed against the portals of Salem. The regime undertook to install a Kommisar. I can say emphatically, as the representative of the regime responsible for direction of the secondary schools, that we would have preferred not to have had to install a Kommissar. I will leave the question of whether this was justified to the judgement of posterity. Meantime the revolution has become an accomplished fact and it is therefore time to close a chapter here and begin a new era. It was for this reason that the regime found it neccessary to ask the school to search for a new director as a successor to Herrn Hahn. The regime has supported the efforts of the school which has finally settled on Herrn Dr. Mittelstrass as the right man, and I can only say that the regime recognizes in him, although he is not a National Socialist, a man suited to be a worthy replacement for Herrn Hahn. I declare now that the regime fully supports the new director and that it must shatter with all its might any sabotage, whether it comes from within or outside the school. The new director must have complete freedom of action and the regime will not impede him in this respect.

"On the other hand it is obvious that the the new regime will make its demands to the new director, and Herr Mittelstrass has guaranteed us that any demands of the new regime will be thoroughly executed. I believe that this solution would not have been achieved for a long time, if the Kommissar Herr Dir. Müller had not in his tactful way prepared the ground in advance.

"But I have also to express a criticism. I am surprised that there are here only eight to ten members of the SA and about eighteen Stahlhelmers. I must tell you something: you have always held England as an ideal. Excuse me. Imagine England in a situation similar to that of Germany. England struck down, humiliated by its enemies, and then—at last a movement for national freedom, proposing to make an end to all this supression and wretchedness—I am certain that not one English youth would be found who.... Here in Salem that is not the case. It would really be rewarding to think it over again. Another example: a few weeks ago I was in Italy, to look at the German school in Milan; without my saying a word the German boys and girls came to me and implored me to start a Hitler Jugend group. They joined to a man. Here is a difference that strikes you in the face, and that perhaps is the underlying explanation of the absence of a bond between you and the people outside. Everywhere you will find that the people are sympathetic to the new times, everywhere you will see the Hitler salute. Here this has not been realized. This antithesis between inside and outside must be eliminated. That will be the assignment of the new director.

[Added in pencil]: "I wish the school a resurrection. May it grow, bloom and flourish. Let it be a model school, not only in the old sense, but also in the sense of the new German Reich. With that thought let us join in a threefold: Sieg Heil!"

By odd chance I have had an independent report on that German school in Milan which the Ministerialrat compared so favorably with Salem. Not long ago I was introduced to a neighbour in Maryland, Dick Metcalf, who had been a junior at Hohenfels a year before my time. Since he was then fluent in German, when his parents moved to Milan in 1935 they enrolled him in the German school. By his account, heaven and hell hardly encompass the contrast between these two schools: "Pictures of der Führer and Hakenkreuze abounded. Among the most asinine courses was Rassenkunde which propounded the insane theory of the superiority of the Aryan race." He adds however that the Ministerialrat was dissembling about the conditions in 1933 when, according to classmates, few even among the German students were seduced by the Hitler Jugend.

After the new Director had been introduced by the Ministerialrat, Mittelstrass also addressed the school assembly [35]:

"Comrades:

"I have been called to this post by the Baden administration and the Herrn Markgraf. I don't come as an outsider; ten years ago I taught here for a year, and a year ago I founded the youngest of the Salem schools, Birkelhof. My purpose in coming here is to initiate a period of quiet and business-like activity, but not a period of cloistered tranquility or a blissful island in a sea of fire—but rather so that the wind that is scouring Germany may also be felt here. We will open ourselves to this wind in the sense that all people do who today are stirred to create something out of this chaos which is consistent with the soul of German history—the dawning of the day of the German people!!!

"You are leaving on vacation now—distance yourselves from the past. Reflect, come back with good spirit, new confidence and your old love of Salem. I am convinced that we will work together and achieve the goal placed before us through the trust of the regime.

"In this sense: Heil! Heil! Heil!"

The branch which Mittelstrass had founded a year before at Birkelhof had not in fact followed Salem principles, and was soon detached from the other schools. Although written denunciations in the archives were not accessible to me, it is my impression that he had denounced Hahn and had even made accusations of sexual misconduct with students. The schools experienced their greatest peril during the fifteen months that followed, at the end of which this unsavory character was replaced.

At this point Herrn Wutsdorf and Meese disappear. Meissner and Mr. Chew joined Hahn at Gordonstoun school in Scotland, and Frl. Köppen will be headmistress at Spetzgart during my next term. A biographical note [36] reports of Fräulein Ewald: "During the first ten years before she opened Spetzgart in 1929 her duties permeated the whole school. In the morning she rose before the students to milk the cow and attend to the invalids—there was as yet no nurse. Then came classroom (she had taken the civil service exams in geography, chemistry and biology), and in the morning training period she coached the high jump." After she had been dismissed from Spetzgart by the Nazis she stayed on so to speak in exile in Salem, and during the war she collaborated with the Forstrat neighbour, whom she had hoped momentarilly might intervene with the Nazi Kommissar, in preparing a catalogue of uncommon local wildflowers, illustrated with her photographs. Even during the years of exile she kept up an interest in taking students on adventurous tours abroad (she herself had once been an exchange student at Bryn Mawr College)—she took a group to Iceland in 1937, when Germans could not leave the country with more than ten Marks. Before and again after the war she also visited Hahn at Gordonstoun every other year, usually to help produce the Christmas play. She directed Salem for three years when it was revived after the war, and thereafter represented it in a "Conference of Internationally Minded Schools," where her accomplishments won the French "Palme Academique."

At the end of a delighful week at Salem, Tomo and I mailed home a large carton of photocopied documents to be later laboriously translated, and continued on our bicycles around the lake to Lindau, and then steeply up into the Swiss Alps. Before departing, Jocelin took us to lunch in the dining hall at Spetzgart, now a collegiate school for students in their last year, where we were entertained by a somewhat harrassed Mentorin, a young woman from South America, and afterwards shown around by two polished and polite students. Here the main buildings were outwardly just as I had described them sixty years earlier.

A Salem Diary: The Junior School; September 1933 to March 1934

During the summer of 1933 so many parents withdrew their children from the school that when I returned to Spetzgart, after a family holiday at the Brittany seashore, the branches at Hohenfels and Hermansberg had been closed. The top four classes had been moved to Salem, and Spetzgart had become the junior school. Jocelin and Dennis were gone, but there were two new boys from England, one of whom, Prince Philip of Greece, was destined to become the spouse of the British monarch.

The Oberterzia class, the one ahead of mine that contained my best friends, was now the oldest at Spetzgart, as I noted with dismay in the first diary entry:

> *The school is full of awful little shrimps. I don't think there will be any more sailing. After lunch the marvelous sport conisted of marching around the playfield under a new teacher who is an SA.*

The new teacher, Nazi Kommissar Flierl, was in charge of *Wehrsport* exercises for the Jungvolk (ages 10 to 14), but the regime was more preoccupied with the older boys eligible for the Hitler Jugend and the SA, and Spetzgart (under Fräulein Köppen who had been reinsated after her furlough) was spared the bitter battles at Salem that characterized the next two terms. The improbable combination of the oafish Herr Flierl, the fuss-budget Fräulein Köppen, and my demotion to a junior school, fused into a highly negative picture which I understood as representing the new German regime. I blamed the Nazis for these misfortunes.

After the first day I persuaded Fräulein Köppen to let me move back to a room with my old friends, Jobst and Breitling. Breitling also had a radio, a great rarity.

> *Fräulein Köppen has made a lot of crazy rules about radio playing,*

I reported.

> *We have to buy a magazine and pick out a few programs of political or musical value and then ask permission from the teacher on duty. Hitler has forbidden jazz but you can hear lots of it from England. Our room is full of wires and aerials. Also you can be sent to jail in Germany if you listen to Moscow. And also if you don't pay two marks every month to the government for listening.*

Fräulein Köppen promptly revealed that, in contrast to her predecessor, she would take personal charge of every detail of the boys' school life. Although not yet eligible, according to the rules, I was granted the privilege of wearing the school uniform. New rules forbade putting your hands in your pockets, along with standing in the hall or courtyard, or keeping any money or food. Compliance must have been incomplete because a week later all pockets were ordered to be removed from the uniforms. "The Köpsch" [the nickname by which the the boys called her], took sole charge of reading aloud to everyone in the rest period after lunch. There was a detailed plan for the arrangement of clothes in the lockers,

> *which Köpsch or someone marks every day as to neatness.*

I noted missing sport periods because of being required to correct deficiencies detected in my Schrankordnung. A comb and hairbrush inspection after supper was supervised by the Schwester, but when she and I could not agree on the outcome I was sent off to clean the comb again under the eyes of the Köpsch. Reviewing her policies thirty years later [36] she still gave top priority to *Schrankordunung:* "Clear and easily monitored tidiness in the clothes lockers is extraordinarily important."

The Training Plan had been introduced at Salem as a way to bind students by trust through a daily incentive to self-supervision and had originated in Hahn's sense of the danger of self-deception and the importance of learning to recognize one's own weaknesses. The student was to prepare a calendar where, with a plus or minus, daily compliance with the series of rules or duties (which I listed in Chapter 1) could be recorded, unchecked by anyone else. The Köpsch drastically rervised both the duties and the element of self-supervision.

> *After supper Fräulein Köppen held another conference in which she did all the talking and another set of laws were drawn up. We will get our pocket money but it sure won't do much good. First we have to pay five pfennigs every time we cross a field which is a shortcut*

> *to Überlingen, next five pfennigs every time we sing a wrong word in singing, and now again every three times we have some clothes lying around in the Duschraum. If so much as a school book or ruler is found in your room even if it is in your table you have to pay five pfennigs. Then it is practically forbidden to lend any clothes, to have any kind of food in the building, to play cards, if your towel happens to fall off its hook you have to pay five pfennigs, and in fact I can't see anything left you can do.*

Three weeks later the training plan was further changed so that, except for punctuality, the occupants of each room would all be jointly penalized for the fault of any one of them.

> *The Zimmer Plan is a thing Köpsch said we have to have every day including Sunday. It is for the whole room as one. A few of the things are window open, bed laid out, shoes out, heat off,* Ordnung, Ordnung nach umziehen in duschraum *(tidiness after undressing in the wash room) and so forth.*

The Köpsch made one personal tour of the boys' *duschraum* or washroom, where no female staff member had ever ventured. She lingered for some time, commenting on this and that, while the more or less naked boys stood around aghast. Stopping by my little revolving basin, she asked whether it was true as appeared that I had only one washcloth: "Do you mean you use the same one for your face and your *niedrigen teilen* (lower parts)?" she asked, snorting in disapproval and tossing her head. After she departed dire threats of personal violence were heard on all sides, should the visit ever be repeated.

All this was a stunning come down after the days of Herr Wutsdorf and Mr. Chew, and the benevolent camp counselor milieu generated by the older Helper and Color-bearer boys, a melancholy contrast to memories of sailing on the lake. One misty September Sunday the Guardian Hans Jahn even let Jobst and me join the seniors sailing a Cutter. There was much horseplay between us and the Godenwind, culminating in everybody's rocking Mr. Chew down from the mast top where he had climbed to take pictures with a camera we had borrowed from Strauss.

The fines that the Köpsch substituted for self-supervision were donated to the *Winterhilfe*. Under the Nazis, contributions to this winter relief charity became virtually compulsory. Refusing to contribute could result in losing one's job for "conduct hostile to the *Volksgemeinschaft*". "Growing unemployment and poverty made hardship during the first winter under the Nazis even more severe than in the preceding depression years, and this was reflected by increased austerity in school meals. Sausage or herring supplemented our sauerkraut only once a week, and we had a white lard-like substitute for butter on our bread, which I tried to toast by putting it on the steam radiators.

> *Sometimes the suppers are not even half as big as American breakfasts. This evening we had cold spaghetti and salad which they protest is watercress but looks suspiciously like weeds. The boys are getting hungry and almost every night a raiding party goes down to the kitchen. They seem to be successful because the teachers are always eating in the living room after they have eaten our supper with us.*

Apples, stored along with other produce from the Markraf's estate in the basement, became less appetizing in the course of the long winter. One evening, to protest, I brought out a pair of scissors to cut mine with. I became instantly subdued when Herr Fischer, who was presiding over my table at dinner, observed this without comment, rose to his feet and departed. The Köpsch sentenced me to "arrest," twenty four hours solitary confinement in the attic with bread and water.

Another punishment devised by the Köpsch was prompted by my erratic attendance at the despised Latin tutoring sessions I continued to have every afternoon after tea with Frau Schraube, at the Inn where she and her husband lived at some distance from the school. One day shortly before the appointed time there was an urgent summons to see the Köpsch. I was ordered to run all the way to the Gasthaus zum Schlössle, half way down to Überlingen, accompanied by another boy who would then confirm that I had indeed run all the way.

> *The lesson was only a half hour which hardly seemed to pay for a half hour's running, and afterwards I had to run all the way up again to meld myself by Köpsch's deadline.*

This punishment at least smacked more of Salem principles, as when later at Gordonstoun some seniors who took a master's car for a 30 mile midnight spin were sentenced by Hahn to walk the same distance the next day [4]. Later the tutoring task was delegated to Frau Schraube's husband, one of the staff who had been conspicuous in denouncing Hahn and others to Kommissar Muller. I found him

> *quite nice except for the usual German failing that he thinks his English is marvelous. I think they were very rich and anyway they had a great deal of land in German South Africa which was taken by*

> *the English after the war. He is just finishing a picture of their old estate, and he can paint quite well.*

The Schraubes were now living in a small hotel room adorned with souvenirs of their life in Africa, and their pining for the great estates they had been forced to relinquish only fifteen years before must have resonated with my own longing to be back at my California home.

Fräulein Köppen's benevolence was probably better acknowledged by many younger children who had not come to her by way of the senior school, as suggested by my rather grudging account of her 44th birthday celebration on February 19.

> *Instead of being able to sleep later like on a decent holiday we had to get up a half hour earlier so that we could go out on her porch and sing songs while she was still in bed. At breakfast there were some presents which I think were mostly from other teachers and mostly flower pots. After lunch there were two plays and one operetta. The plays were humorous and the high spots were when a girl accidentally threw a bucket of dirty water all over the teachers in the front row, and when one of the numerous ghosts fell through the curtains on the elevated stage in back. The operetta will be shown again in Salem, and the plays also tomorrow for the children in Hödingen.*

In this village a mile north of Spetzgart there was evidently either a school for poor local children, or perhaps an orphanage.

Herr Meese had complained of lack of discipline at Spetzgart when he adressed a school assembly in June, as acting Director while Frls. Ewald and Köppen and others had been furloughed by the Nazi Kommissar. Perhaps because of this the Köpsch was now a bit more of a martinet than she had been as head of the now closed junior Hermansberg branch, although it was on staff rather than on students that Meese had actually been concerned to inflict discipline and adherance to Nazi guidance. But, reading her obituary notice [36], I see that some of my impressions may not have been far off he mark. "From the beginning the nine to thirteen-year-olds were entrusted to her. The energetic teacher was always a match for this noisy, restless contingent. She knew all the vulnerable points in the childrens' daily lives, from regular washing and cold showers to table manners and regular clothing changes."

But my notion that she somehow represented the educational ideas of the new regime was indeed mistaken. At a talk he gave for his 80th birthday celebration Hahn described her as the "undissuadable, the unyielding—the Nazis would have said: the uneducable." The record shows that, although she continued teaching unlike others who had been furloughed in June, she was the object of so many denunciations in the following years that in 1937 she had to leave Spetzgart for the branch which had by then reopened at Hermannsberg and which, being in a different province, provided a refuge from her Nazi enemies in the Baden administration. Jocelin told me that once, late in the day, when confronted by a very high ranking Nazi official who asked her if she could not agree that some single good thing had stemmed from his regime, she answered: "What is rotten at the roots can bear no fruit." This simple answer haunts me a bit, as I know that I could not then have answered as well, and can not do so today. The school had been her whole life. In her last testament she wrote [36]: "Listen to your teachers and attend to them, for they look after your souls, for doing which they are accountable."

The Köpsch was not the kind of person whom Hahn would have sought out for the senior school. Many bitter conflicts with the regime in the years ahead were over what I would call not so much the principles of Salem as school traditions, such as the Christmas play which was prohibited as ideologically unacceptable; I expect it was often disputes over such issues that prompted denunciations against her.

She was famous for the imaginative room decorations that celebrated the weeks before Christmas. On Nov. 26th I wrote:

> *The last three weeks of the term they call Adventszeit. Every room is supposed to be decorated by its occupants with some scene out of Christ's life. What we are going to have is a sail boat on the water and then the pier coming from the land which goes up a hill on the top of which is the Krypta (house with the Christ child in it) and the three kings and a lot of angels and sheep and Joseph and Mary.*

The sailboat in a harbour at Bethlehem was obviously my inspiration, and I spent a week restoring a three-foot model of a four-masted clipper that had been abandoned in the paint room.

> *The masts were gone and Herr Fischer said it was hopeless but I didn't pay any attention to him. I sharpened the lower end of the upper masts and made a slit in the bottom ones but that didn't hold so I filed off the heads of nails and put them in which worked very well.*

The landscape was built up with fir branches and moss and moss-covered stones and twigs for trees, and I can smell today the fragrance of fir branches that filled the whole building. Prizes were awarded after the judges toured all the rooms.

Ours is about third best and Sean's (my brother had transferred to Spetzgart with the Köpsch) room was the best in the old building.

In spite of shadows there were cheerful moments during these terms. After a lecture by Kommissar Flierl, Hindenburg's birthday was celebrated by a twenty mile walking tour that went to Ludwigshafen at the western tip of the Bodensee, by ferry to the south shore, then past the ruin of a "lovely old castle" to Mindelsee pond for a swim (where we ran into the Jung Volk group who said they were having a hard time under Herr Flierl), and finally by another ferry back to Überlingen. Along the way Jobst and I eluded our own tour leader long enough to persuade a farmer to give us some *Most* (new wine) from his huge wine barrels.

Fräulein Köppen went with our group as an observer but I don't think she ever will again. At the last ferry she was too far behind to wait for.

Another October Sunday was enlivened, after the Köpsch had directed me to stay at school and study, when a man and his little boy offered Jobst and me a ride in the rumble seat of their car that was

so tiny that the lausbub *could have pushed it as fast as he can walk around the Hof. We went to see a big Nazi training exhibition. One bunch ran off with lamps in different directions and signaled each other, and others were hiding in bushes with machine guns that were supposd to be invisible but tan and orange shows up marvelously against green. The best though was a group laying a telephone wire. They ran along at an awful speed and fastened it around evey tree. The man who owned the car knew the head man who was an admiral in the war I think and who was covered with badges and so forth. When we got back the Köpsch was very mad but couldn't do anything about it.*

In a 1934 talk introducing Salem to an English audience [11] Hahn had mentioned that "Expeditions to and fro to rob and rag the rival [branch] were planned and dreamed of for months beforehand, many of them, thank Heaven, not coming off, but some I am afraid carried out with strategical genius and tactical precison in the early hours of the morning." On January 25th we woke to find the school pitch dark. True to tradition, a group of Salem seniors had come in a car while we were sleeping, entered the dining room through a window, unscrewed and hidden all the fuses and concealed the cups and spoons someplace in the grounds. After breakfast of mush eaten with forks, retaliatory plans were solicited at an assembly, and after a few impractical proposals by the boys

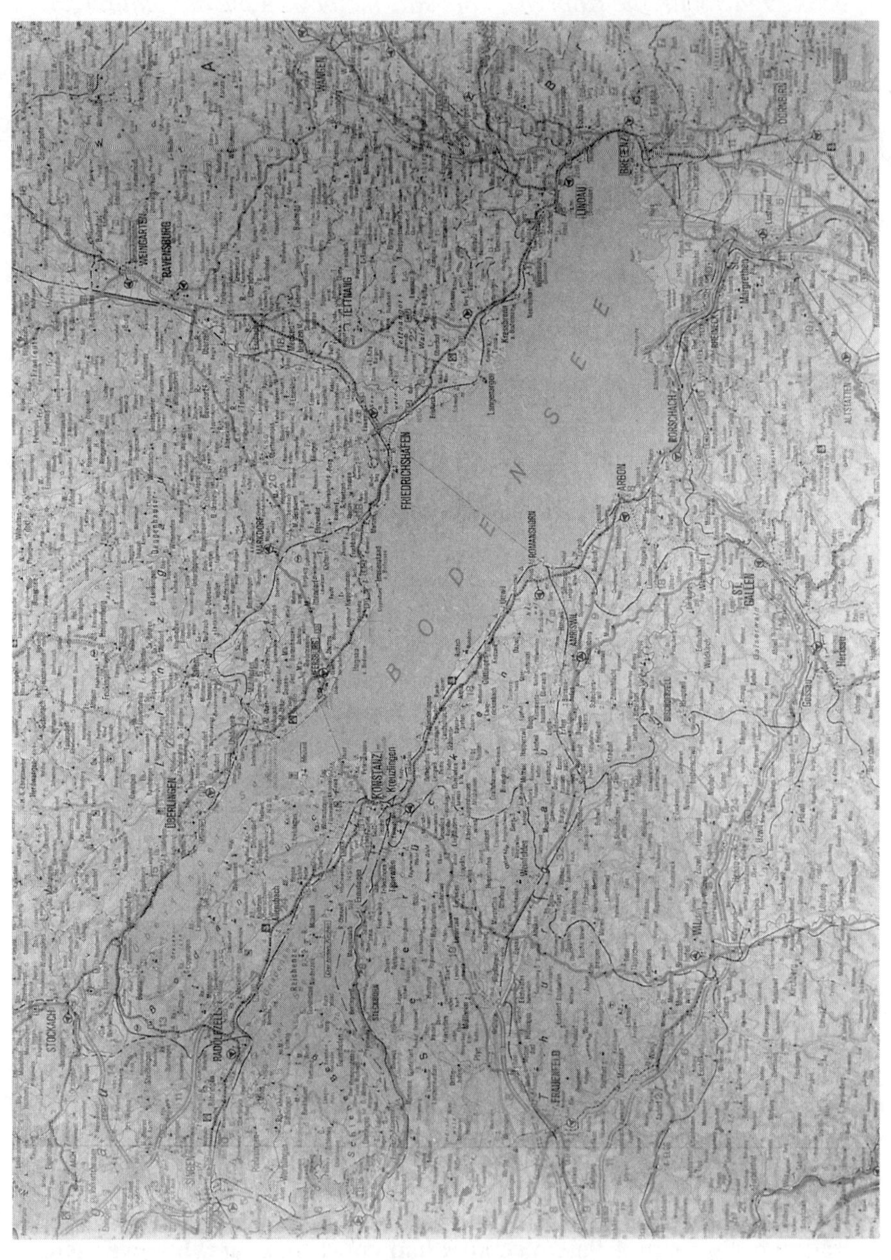

Map of the Bodensee, illustrating sailing, walking and bicycle tours described in Chapters 4 and 6.

Frl. Köppen decided that all eighty of us should go to Salem around six o'clock while they were having study period and ensconce ourselves in the dining hall, so that by the time they got there their suppers would have been consumed. After a day of fruitless search for the missing items the whole school boarded a train and, arriving after dark found everything awfully well locked up, but Philip had some special keys that let us in by a side gate. The plan succeeded in so far as as we persuaded the kitchen staff to start serving us the evening meal before the Salemers arrived in sufficient numbers to evict us. But back at Spetzgart we found that

> *the Salemers had been there again and overpowered the tiny guard we had left and taken the butter and cheese. However this didn't matter because it is mostly the teachers that get it. The Germans call this kind of thing a* Streich.

The great Water Bomb War in October was memorable to me because of being a rare moment when I felt something of my own self as an American had managed to surface and catch its breath out of the German sea.

> *There is now a war of the Oberterzia against the Unterterzia although other people take part by just shooting at anyone with slingshots and water bombs. I learned how to make water bombs four years ago. I almost forgot about them until one day I made a couple and showed Jobele how.*

It was a way of folding paper into a container that would hold water long enough to drop from a window onto a passing enemy below.

> *They are being used with good effect here now.*

The fights, which continued for several days,

> *are usually the Oberterzia getting into a classroom and piling all the tables and chairs against the door, and the Unterterzia trying to get in or keep them from getting out.*

At one point I managed to cross a roof and get in through a window. After they closed it,

> *Prince Philip pushed so hard he knocked it in and our side could shoot slingshots through the hole as much as we liked. Windows are broken here now at an average of six a day and they are great big expensive ones too.*

On the third day Fräulein Köppen announced the water bomb war would continue all day but only on the sport field, and after that there would be a big bonfire and all the slingshots and water bombs would be thrown into it to signal the end of the war.

Before Christmas I noted that at a school assembly

> *The Köpsch told us about the children in the Hödinger school. We are to divide into groups of two and three to make presents for them. She talked a lot about how they want toys rather than practical things. But there was one boy thirteen who is supposed to be quite poor, so Philip and I went together as between us we have four pairs of shoes all too small. Also we went to the Schreinerei to make a puzzle and another game called 'fifteen.' The puzzle was easy enough, but when it came to the box and all the little pieces for the 'fifteen' we consistently made mathematical mistakes, but at last very late we finished. The next morning I got Köpsch to let me into the Schreinerei and worked on a new 'fifteen' game as the one Philip made* [he now gets full credit] *was terrible. After that Philip and I decided to make a small bowling game, the kind with nine sticks and a ball. We got into the paint room through a window and painted them and then punched holes in a can of paint that was like putty and threw it out the window.*

Later:

> *After supper quite a few of us went to Hödingen to see the Christmas we gave the children there and it was very nice.*

The Philip who has begun to appear in the preceding accounts of "cheerful moments" was Philip of Greece, today the spouse of the English monarch. The German boys called him "Greece" but, as with other English-speaking boys, I called him by his first name. His sister Theodora had been married for two years to the Markgraf Berthold at the time Philip came to Salem. I noted his arrival three days into the term, but apparently did not get to know him quickly or well because he was reintroduced six weeks later:

> *There are two boys here who can speak good English and they are both very nice. One is called Philip of Greece, he is the Prince of Greece and is about my age.*

Actually Philip had little connection with Greece. His father had been banished in the chaos that followed the disastrous attempt after the war to reclaim Greek enclaves from Turkey in Asia Minor, and had taken Danish citizenship. Philip's parents became estranged after a few years in France, and during his early formative years he had been shuttled about among his mother's aristocratic relatives in England, while his father and sisters remained closer to their German connections. The other three sisters also married German aristocrats who, like the Markgraf, had legally but not effectively lost their titles with the fall of the Kaiser. Of these, the husband of the youngest, Sophie, was a dedicated Nazi appointed by Goering to be head of the precursor of the *Geheime Staatspolizei*, or Gestapo. Later Sophie's second marriage was to Prince George of Hanover, a senior at Salem during my time, who was to serve as Headmaster after the war.

Philip was also in the Unterterzia but in the classical curriculum.

> *After breakfast the U III Humana challenged us to a cavalry fight. Our class is smaller anyway and half of it is girls so we didn't have much chance. There were four riders and horses on each side. I was on Knoll against Philip on Niko. I almost pulled Philip off and then he got back on and I kicked Knoll in the leg by accident or something and he fell down but even then Philip fell right on top of us.*

Another day when

> *it was raining and muddy so the only sport was walking Philip and I had to wax floors because we slid around on them in the living room. As Köpsch wasn't there we pretended to* bohnen *(wax) but just threw the mops at whoever came by.*

And another:

> *Sunday morning Philip and I wanted to go to Friedrichshafen* (home port for the Graf Zeppelin) *but it was a* fest tag *and Köpsch said too serious for bummling around in the streets, so we went to see the aircraft lookout. They made a sort of big pit with boards on all sides of it out of which they can shoot with antiaircraft guns or machine guns I guess. Then we came back very slowly discussing an idea for a giant yoyo which would be worked from the Graf Zeppelin. Inside would be a man with a machine gun who would shoot into the windows as it went down and then they would pull it up again to the Zeppelin.*

Philip was a year younger than I, but I thought of him at the time as older as well as more adventurous. One night around bed time he came by with a flashlight and enlisted me to spy on the girls' dorm from a large outdoor deck at the end of he hall. Sure enough, from the end of the deck one could look down the length of the old wing, where presently the flashlight attracted shadows of girls to the windows. Soon after, several actual figures of what seemed in the darkness to be truly huge girls appeared in the doorway to our deck. In the corner of the deck there was a folded canvas stool about two feet square, and Philip instantly proposed hiding beind it. It looked ridiculously small. I hesitated and the opportunity was lost.

The Markgraf had urged his wife to enroll her brother in Salem for leverage in his battles with the Nazi regime; it still valued the school for its ties to England at a time when English parents, and many German parents as well, were withdrawing their children. Philip's brief stay there seems to have contributed disproportionately to the German popular image of the school ever since. Last summer when our bicycle club was touring from Munich to Venice the group included a woman near my age who had grown up in Überlingen. Her only response to my questions about townspeoples' views of the school next door was "Royalty! Prince Philip!"

Prince Philip left Germany when Gordonstoun opened in 1934. According to a recent biography by Denis Judd he served at Gordonstoun as color bearer and Helper and was appointed Guardian in his fifth year. Echoing my own experience at Spetzgart, his greatest enthusiasm was for sailing, now in rough seas more challenging than the Bodensee. Philip came to excell at the high jump at Gordonstoun. Hahn's view of the special powers of this exercise received fateful confirmation when, shortly after graduation, Philip was first introduced to his future wife, the thirteen-year-old Princess Elizabeth. After he had displayed his prowess on this occasion by jumping over a tennis net, the Princess's nanny, Miss Crawford, found that her charge had been impressed: "Lilibet said, 'How good he is Crawfie! How high he can jump!'"

I have no memory of field hockey being played at Spetzgart, but wherever Hahn was this game was in the forefront. A hockey team had been formed at Salem in 1919 even six months before the school opened, with Prince Max in goal and Frl. Ewald at center half, and later when Hahn ran into a forlorn, newly enrolled Jocelin Winthrop-Young he had promised him a hockey stick if he could memorize a poem in German. Memories of the forgotten promise may color Jocelin's later account of field hockey at Gordonstoun [7]: "Hahn had played hockey with some success at Oxford and always wore his Christchurch colours when playing. At Gordonstoun he still played outside right in the team. A boy always accompanied him just outside the touchline, with a thermos flask of coffee. From time to time he would stop playing and refresh himself with a gulp or two. Then he might have to speed back into the game to reach a pass coming his way. In 1936 I was elected hockey captain and, after a short trial period, dropped him from the team. After all he was fifty years old! He never forgot this and often recalled: 'My boy, I knew immediately the vote was finished that I was out!' No doubt he forgave me. But twenty years later after I had played in a match in Salem he wrote in his critique: 'At center half our guest from Greece drifted over the center field like a gentle South Wind.'"

After the war Hahn was asked by Reuters to write a press release about Philip's school days, at the time the royal enagement was announced [38]. The press release successfully avoided sycophantic praise: "His best is outstanding, his second best is not good enough." But in reviewing his athletic achievements it cites captaincy of the first hockey team, noting that though "not fast enough to excel among his contemporaries he was chosen captain because he could lead a team." Jocelin told me that he sought Hahn out soon after this appeared in the press and reminded him with some indignation that it was he, not Philip, who had been hockey captain. To this Hahn's rather splendid reply was: "My boy, you are completely wrong."

The most fateful and ominous change in school life was embodied in the appearance of a full time Nazi Kommissar whose visible function was to lead the Hitler Jungvolk contingent and supervise Wehrsport and close-order drill for all the boys. No doubt he was also there to report ideological deviations, but his achievement in that direction was not dramatic enough to earn mention in the school archives. Short, pudgy, balding, usually without his SA uniform, to our eyes aged and decrepit (he might have been thirty), a transmutated lausbub, Herr Flierl seemed out of his element and ill-suited to sway youth to his cause. All the boys called him "Congo." Like the Führer, he was a painter. He brought his brushes to school assemblies, and would occupy himself painting völkisch scenes on what appeared to be little eight inch squares of window glass. Fruitless pursuits of one or another young woman also often distracted his attention from us.

Herr Flierl supervised close-order drill every Monday afternoon. After two months the monotony was relieved:

> *in Wehrsport we started something new which is at least a little better than just marching. It is like when charging another trench. Geting up, running, falling down again and so forth.*

Another day he

> *divided us up into groups and said we should play leapfrog. We jumped all over he place and everyone got knocked flat including Herr Flierl so he stopped it and we had to make a* dauerlauf *(long distance run).*

Gordonstoun field hockey team in the thirties. Standing: Kurt Hahn, far right; Jocelin Winthrop Young, second from left. Kneeling, Prince Philip, far left. The picture must have been taken shortly before Jocelin dropped the headmaster from the team. Below: Prince Philip enrolling Prince Charles at Gordonstoun, and Hahn encouraging the tennis players.

Occassionally there were more entertaining war games.

> *After lunch there was a Kriegspiel* [war game] *in which eighteen boys from the higher grades played against the same number from the Spetzgart Jungvolk. We went quite far away to a small valley with forested hills on both sides. Each side has a flag and plants it in a circle where it can't be seen in the trees. A person can be dead twice, each time by being hit three times by the same person. The second time he can't play any more. We went up the left side which turned out to be the best, and won by getting both flags in our circle. Because of the Jungvolk not winning Herr Flierl got very mad and said there would be another Kriegspiel the next day.*

The replay pitted the school against the Überlingen Jungvolk, which was to come up from town and try to capture Spetzgart.

> *Forty of us climbed to the top of the hill in back of Spetzgart where Herr Flierl made elaborate preparations. He sent off three Spee troups in different directions, who were to send a messenger back if they found the enemy or anyway when the bugle blew. They all worked fine except where the enemy went through and there the messengers couldn't get back because the enemy had passed them before they noticed it. When messengers from the other Gruppen came back and said they had seen nothing we were getting suspicious so Herr Flierl ordered* hinlegen *[lie down] and everone looked up and down the opposite hills. Although bunches of cows were seen I don't think anyone once saw a Jungvolker. In fact despite all the elaborate Spee troups the actual defenders were the first ones to see the advancing army. Bulle said he was just pulling out his field glasses to look for them when they grabbed him (he is a little short-sighted). We didn't see them until they were a couple of hundred yards away and then we had to run down to the Hof. About twenty were sent off in various directions so when we fell in there were about fifteen of us against seventy five of them when they began pouring down the hill and crossing the road. We threw dirt and stones to try to stop them from getting up the other hill but they came up anyway. They were smaller than we but pretty ferocious. They pull at your hair and knife you and everything. Then the whistle blew and we all went up to the Hof where they fell in and stood up their two machine guns (which luckily were wooden) and I counted them to make sure they were seventy five.*

We were assembled on several occasions to listen to Hitler's radio talks. In November *there was a speech by Hitler which we heard over the radio. It was a bad radio and I couldn't understand hardly anything. He talked pretty well though and it would have made an awful lot of noise if the radio had been strong enough. He said it was the part of every single person in Germany to help the new Regime on to success. I think he said some other thing about France too after which they all yelled.*

Again in January,

Hitler made a long speech at the opening of the Reichstag and the first anniversary of the Hitler regime. We heard it with my radio which I took down to the living room. I didn't understand much except that Austria always had been German and if there were Nazis in it who wanted it to be again why it was quite natural.

Martial spirit blossomed the next month:

The boys have an awful lot of tear gas pistols. One of them in our class put a shell on the radiator and it melted from the heat which is the same as shooting it. In a few minutes it was all over the room and it not only brings the tears to your eyes so that you can't see but burns and smells sweetly. The teacher got awfully mad about it and was afraid to even come in. The Germans seem to think the next war will be fought mostly with gas.

Already from the start of the term there had been in my classroom

a picture of Germany's weapons and soldiers and it is sure exaggerated. Germany had two soldiers and one gun and France had at least fifty soldiers and piles of guns, twenty airplanes and twenty tanks, and Poland almost as much as France.

At the start of the term I noted that

there is Wehrsport every Monday and now the foreigners have to do it too.

Some time later, when we were all assembled outdoors in military formation, Herr Flierl made a speech announcing that in view of the situation in the new Reich, any foreigners who felt it inappropriate to continue participating were invited to step out of the ranks, and would be assigned to some unspecified alternative activity. Philip, who was very blond (I had light hair at that age too) turned and said to me "I am going to be *feige* [cowardly; he was being facetious] in the eyes of

Herr Flierl." It seemed equally certain to me that the alternative activity would prove to be grossly inferior.

While Herr Flierl waited expectantly for his racial lesson to unfold, one by one about half a dozen boys dropped out of the ranks and stood in front of us. A swarthy small Italian typified the straggling group. The last, after long hesitation, was the German Jewish boy Strauss. The blond Nordic foreigners had stayed in the ranks. Before dismissing us Herr Flierl paced back and forth a bit, glowing with pride at the outcome of his object lesson. As I recall, Strauss was a sensitive, bright and physically awkward boy. On one occasion he had joined Jobst and I to visit the Schwaben, in its Überlingen dock, when a sudden storm put the small craft off shore in distress.

> *Strauss got so interested that he went farther and farther down the stone slip until he got to the moss. Then he started to slip and he went up to his ankles where by staying perfectly still and yelling he didn't go any further. When we were able to stop laughing we pulled him up again."*

I must have tarried somewhere, because when I reached the school Hof or courtyard the ensuing episode was in full swing. Strauss was running about with a big wicker waste paper basket over his head, inside a wide circle of the younger boys who were pushing and taunting him. Outside the circle where I stood with the older boys who were not participating, I asked what was going on: Strauss was guilty of *selbsterniedrigung*. He had debased himself because he was German (although Jewish), and only foreigners had been offered the choice of dropping out. Why did not Strauss throw off the waste basket? What was going on? It was obvious that he was actually being bullied because he was Jewish (and timid). Herr Fisher, the only staff member present, appeared to be wavering back and forth outside the circle. He had never been seen as indecisive before, certainly not when I cut the apple with scissors at dinner. Soon now he was beganing to look unmanned rather than indecisive. I had never seen a teacher who did not know whether he or a gang of ten-year-olds was the boss.

Of the school I was at when I was nine years old I remember nothing but the name. Sean remembers the above episode of the wicker basket. Only after that a few other things. Resolving not to give the Hitler salute when all the other boys did as a parade passed by, the twenty mile walk around the lake, and the raid on Salem. He remembers that we lost the war with Salem! They just threw us out after we sat down in their dining room. I see that my diary describes it that way too but then—it waffles, it implies we just went home and said we won. Now I see also that a little self-deception, Hahn's bête noir, has faithfully accompanied me all the years since—about the importance of my scientific discoveries, and of this book you are reading.

I might note here in connection with Sean's memories that a reason given for Philip's removal from Salem soon after was that [38] "Whenever the Nazi salute was given he roared with laughter. His sister thought it better for him, and also for them, if he returned to England right away." The Hitler greeting had become compulsory for public employees in July 1933.

Throughout these terms Jobst Frowein continued to be my best friend as he had been at the beginning.The kinds of things we did were not always impeccable examples of the Salem spirit of learning through adventure. As an example, on a week-end when the Köpsch gave us permission to hike through through the Hödinger Tobel to Sipplingen, we went instead to a farmhouse in Hödingen to visit a former Spetzgart nurse.

> *Jobst wanted to ask Mami about his knee which had gone out. The Schwester we have at Spetzgart is from Hermannsberg and not only a very bad Schwester but very tough. Köpsch brought her because the old one was too nice for the* lausbubs *in Spetzgart. She lives in what I suppose is a typical German village house. It sure was primitive although very neat and clean.*

From this my only glimpse of the other world next door I remember a ship's ladder up to a loft from the middle of the room, wooden benches and stools, lots of leather harnesses and such on the walls.

> *We only saw one room which is her children's room and living room and the sleeping room for everyone. Here we sat down and she told Jobst that what the other Schwester was doing was all wrong but she couldn't do anything about it because Köpsch would be terribly mad if she found out that anyone from Spetzgart went to some other Schwester. Then she started talking and she is quite a gossiper. First she told us why Herr Wutsdorf left. Because the older boys were mean to him all the time. They were egged on by Fräulein Rokol. She was mad at Herr Wutsdorf because she wanted to marry him and he said no. Now she was going around with Herr Flierl lately.*

After this new perspective on the story of Herr Wutsdorf, she continued with an interesting account of some recent public afffairs.

> *Then she told us a lot about when the Nazis drove out or killed the*

Communists. It seems she was living with her husband in the city that was the center of the red forces. They came into the houses and commandeered the people around and made them all sleep on straw as they wanted the beds for themselves. They were lucky, however, in being able to hide the whiskey as otherwise the reds would have been sure to get very drunk. That night the Nazi troops came in and in one minute all the reds had completely disappeared. Then she told us about hearing the Reichstag fire trial on the radio and how dumb Dimitroff was when he yelled at the judges and how Lubbe just pretended he was in a coma and when they yelled at him he forgot to hold his head downwards. She said the officials had to clean his nose for him.

After that she told about how terrible the schools in the smaller towns were and how if she went back to Berlin she was going to tell the Reichstag about it. She says the teacher in Hödingen has almost killed several pupils and that you can hear his yelling for miles around. I don't think they have any orphan homes in Germany, but anyway the town gets full of children without parents. These children are divided among the farmers, and she said some of the farmers make them get up at three in the morning, work until school and afterwards till supper like animals while they themselves lie in bed and this also she intends to tell the Reichstag.

The only memory I have of the Spetzgart Schwester in her capacity as nurse is of compulsory visits to have glycerine rubbed on our ankles in winter. Hahn is said to have taken charge aggresively in cases of serious illness: he would cause a doctor a great deal of woe if he felt any doubt of his ministrations, and knew where all the best specialists were to be found and how to get them interested—except for psychiatrists, whom he thoroughly distrusted. Golo Mann indicts Hahn for believing emotional difficulties could be overcome by will power, and cites his comment after a student suicide that the boy had given him his "word of honour" that he would not do it [39]. Fair criticism, but Mann may estimate the successes of psychiatry more highly than others have done. When, a few months after Freud's only visit to America, the professors at Clark University where he had lectured began to write him about their disappointing results with his therapy, his reply was limited to "showing me something that's working better."

"Scarlet Fever and Quarantine." The diary thus announces a medical drama that occupied the last weeks of my year at Spetzgart.

All the children that don't live here had to go home right away. The

> *rest of us were directed to go outside and have a game of Indians against Trappers. When we got back everything had been cleaned and all the clothes we had on were put in the laundry. Also there was a huge ambulance there. The teachers that don't live in Spetzgart weren't allowed to come up any more.*

Our headmistress came through this crisis with imagination and flying colors. For the last two weeks of thc term she let the survivors prepare a performance of *Wilhelm Tell* by Schiller.

> *It is all poetical and so of course everything has to be learnt by heart.*

CHAPTER 7

Salem, 1933 to 1945: Strategies for Survival in the Third Reich

In July 1933, after a newly appointed Kommissar had suspended a number of the senior staff, Ministerialrat Kraft had undertaken to reorganize the Salem schools, and he chose as the new Director Mittelstrass, a shifty character prominent among those who had secretly denounced Hahn. During the following terms, in contrast to the relative tranquility in the Junior school at Spetzgart, Director Mittelstrass at Salem was continuously in conflict wih the old staff and above all with Erich Meissner, Hahn's supporter who had written a circular letter to the parents at the time of Hahn's arrest in March.

In a tribute to Meissner long afterward [10] Hahn quoted his friend's remarks at a school assembly in November; this may convey the flavor of the earlier letter. "Our people have been given a warning.... German education has the mission, and if it chooses also the power, to intervene at this point and to counteract a deep seated corruption and human paralysis and degeneration. Salem's contribution to the nation lies in this knowledge and this duty.... Never, and not even at the moment of greatest national intoxication, is there a time that allows us respite from the demands of our own conscience or absolves us from the inflexible duty to intercede for what we perceive to be right; no less if this should bring us into conflict with our fellow countrymen, or if in consequence we are ostracized or placed in the greatest personal danger. Whoever accustoms himself to feel excused, because others so feel, is corrupted."

In this unqualified defiance of Hitler we hear a voice quite unlike any we have heard before, including that of Hahn himself, who was surely right in adding that Meissner would have paid with his life had he stayed in Germany. Meissner and Frl. Ewald were reinstated after July, and Mittelstrass agreed in September to share jurisdiction with them. But did not keep his word. In April he again broke a promise to put Meissner in charge of "Other Activities," and brought in a Herr Dr. Fluck to try to make the Hitler Jugend dominant over the school.

After the war a staff member reminisced about this era [26]: "[We] undertook to try to remain true to Salem principles while appearing to follow the new regulations, encouraged by the hope that the 'thousand-year Reich' might not last very long. At first we were only asked to set aside a room for the Hitler Jugend, but harmony was not achieved. Some older students belonged to the SA and disregarded school rules about drinking and smoking. Boys were made Führers in the HJ who had not earned any respect in the school body."

Three senior Helpers who joined the HJ at this time and were doing poorly in the classroom, had posted a notice: "Brook no interference from teachers or other students. The whole Party stands behind you." In the final Abitur exams they got a grade of only five in several subjects, which meant automatic disqualification for university admission. However, the Minister of Culture privately proposed that if they made better scores at target practice with firearms, they would receive the gift of passing grades in the Abitur. When the students improved their marksmanship, the Minister changed their failing grades in his own handwriting, after the respective teachers had refused to do so. Complaints about disruption by the HJ could have been heard at almost any German school throughout the next decade. The Nazi leaders' contempt for intellectual achievement endangered their own goals in military technology by populating universities with unprepared students.

A letter to the Markgraf from an alumnus or friend [40] conveys how this year at Salem unfolded:

"Salem appears, after the separation of the non-Aryan Hahn, worth preserving as a bridge to England and as a source of soldierly training. The interest, of the men who make the decisions, in the preservation of Salem was strong enough that in July 1933 Meissner, and in November 1933 Frl. Ewald, were reinstated because they were guarantors of the Salem system. This was a big set back for the local rabble-rousers who were thinking not of the nation or the Party but of their own prestige, which was linked to the destruction of Salem. The interest of the decision-makers in the preservation of Salem flickers only intermittently, but is however strong enough to be revived when Salem is threatened with going under. Such occasions were: In September 1933 when Mittelstrass installed himself as sole ruler, and thereby broke the pledge that had been made to the English and the parents about the division of jurisdictions, and at Easter 1934 when the reinstatement of Meissner, proposed by the school association and solemnly agreed to by Mittelstrass, was denied by Mittelstrass on grounds that amounted to lies and treachery.

"After this nothing could be done: Mittelstrass as a man of unqualified loyalty to the state, and Fluck as sturdy director of military physical training, were all powerful. One could only pray that the inevitable catastrophe would come soon enough for rescue to be possible. This prayer was answered: Fluck was revealed as the inferior person that almost all children and adults, except for Mittelstrass, had already recognized him to be. Mittelstrass had misjudged him, not because he has no sense for uncleanliness and shabby character—on the contrary his sensitivity to this is by nature well developed—but because he wanted to misjudge him because he needed him to paralyze and separate Meissner. Thereby he sacrificed the children to his greed for power. In education that is a mortal sin. Fluck's annihilation disposes of Mittelstrass as director of Salem. It is possible that by now the reinstatement of Meissner and Ewald can not be brought about. But not to propose it would mean for the school that the guilt for its disintegration would be shifted from those that are really at fault to those summoned in its defence. The tragedy of the battle of the Marne lies not in that it was lost but rather in that it was given up for lost before the last chance for victory had been exploited."

As foreseen by the correspondent, Meissner was not reinstated. After a dramatic altercation with Mittelstrass at a staff meeting, he resigned at the end of the summer term, followed by Frl. Ewald. By now he was at real risk. After his November talk a warrant for his arrest had been issued at Karlsruhe. When this was suspended through the unauthorized intervention of Ministerialrat Kraft, local Party officials seriously debated his murder. In July 1934 he managed to cross the Swiss border secretly at night, and joined the teaching staff at Hahn's new school in Scotland. Unlike the Markgraf and Meissner, Hahn himself never considered closing down the school. Even from exile he negotiated in behalf of the school's survival, and persuaded influential compatriots to travel to Gordonstoun, where he tried to enlist them to serve as Director of Salem.

Speaking to an English audience a decade later during the war, Meissner described this period at Salem [16]:

"What happened to Salem after the Headmaster had been expelled? Tribute must be paid to the brave resistance which the responsible Salem boys put up to check the moral deterioration [but] they were fighting a losing battle for it was, of course, impossible that Salem should win through if the Nazis suceeded everywhere else. When we decided in the early summer of 1933 to carry on, it was on the assumption that the final victory of the Nazis was by no means assured. The Nazis were gaining ground every day. The school, however, defended its independence and precariously preserved its inner life for about another year and a half.

"The local SA formations began to consider Salem as a territory that must be conquered and occupied. The permanent threat of arrest, the spying system officially introduced, the the vile tactics of intimidation—all this, though very unpleasant in itself, was not the most serious difficulty. The acute danger always arises from within. Nazi spirit began to invade the school. The main attack of our opponents was an attempt to corrupt the idea of citizenship and transform it into something else —the spirit of the gang combined with adoration of the 'Führer.' Let us leave the puerile cult of the Führer aside; what is the spirit of the gang? Every boy knows—unconditional loyalty to one's fellows. A true citizen who owes allegiance to a common cause will not shelter his fellow who has endangered the cause. He turns against him. His conscience compells him to do so. During the last critical month of Salem's struggle the Nazis were aiming at one object: to discredit citizenship and supplant it by the spirit of the gang. This trick worked, not with many but with some, they began to waver and hesitate and eventually they broke away. The Nazis glorify brutality. The young are easily misled—they become callous and believe that they are strong and bold. There was a case of mob justice in Salem, a new thing. Mob justice is identical in spirit with persecution, therefore it calls for the strongest counteraction. But when the boy who had been the ringleader in this particular case was punished, the local Party authorities interfered and expressed their approval of his behaviour."

This incident may have been the same that Prince Phillip described during the term after I left Spetzgart [1]: "After two terms at Spetzgart I moved to Salem as a junior. Nazi flags started to appear and a number of senior boys joined the Hitler Jugend. Some stuck out against the Nazi takeover and one senior boy in particular, who was responsible for us juniors, so displeased these thugs that they caught him one night and shaved his head. I lent him my old school cricket cap and I hope he has got it still."

Salem's resistance did not end in 1934, as Meissner thought it had from his exile ten tears later. As background, it may be useful to review some salient events of the first year and a half of the Nazi regime. In the first weeks terrorist SA and SS units acting as autonomous police totally and permanently liquidated what had been for seventy years the most coherent working class organization and culture in Europe.Then on February 27 the Reichstag burned. Communists were blamed for arson, but the fire was probably started by the Nazis, and planned so as to take place a week before what was to be the last election (March 5: the Nazi vote increased from 33 to 44%). On February 28 the "Presidential Decree for the Protection of People and State" permitted seizure of power in all provincial governments, and suspended civil rights, authorizing arbitrary search and confiscation of property, the suspension of personal liberty and the right of free expression of opinion including freedom of the press, and the right of assembly and association. This decree authorized Hahn's imprisonment without trial on March 3.

Bands of SA and SS terrorized the country in an orgy of anarchic violence during the following month. With complete disregard for police and higher Nazi authorities Communists and Social Democrats were beaten, tortured, detained in ad hoc concentration camps, and buildings were broken into and vandalized in nightly raids. Small businesses were quickly persuaded to employ an "old fighter" trom the SA for protection, and foreigners thought to look like Jews, and even embassies, were attacked.

Reconvened at Potsdam, the parliament reduced itself to a sounding board on March 24 by passing an "Enabling Law" which allowed Hitler to introduce laws and decrees, and change the constitution, without consulting it. To obtain the needed two thirds votes communist deputies had been imprisoned and the center parties won over by promises and intimidation. One of the 94 Social Democrat deputies who voted against has described this last session of the Reichstag [29]: "At the entrance youths with swastikas on their chests made us run the gauntlet, calling us names like 'Center pig', 'Marxist sow.' In the cloakroom we learned that one of our Party leaders had been arrested on entering the building.The chamber was crawling with armed SA and SS men who lined the exits behind us in a semicircle. Hitler read his declaration. Only in a few places did he raise his voice to a fanatical frenzy: when he demanded the public execution of van der Lubbe (for setting the Reichstag on fire), and when he uttered dark threats of what would happen if the Reichstag did not vote the Enabling Act. We tried to dam the flood of Hitler's unjust accusations with interruptions of 'No!', 'False!' but that did us no good. The SA and SS people, who surrounded us in a semicircle along the walls, hissed loudly and murmured: 'Shut up, Traitors, You'll be strung up today!'."

On April 7th a Law for the Re-establishment of the Civil Service authorized a purge of Jewish and other so-called unreliable teachers from the Public Schools. By the following summer 20 percent of head teachers in secondary schools and 60 percent of lecurers in teachers colleges had been dismissed, as well as 15 percent of University teachers, including 20 past or future Nobel laureates, all but one of whom emigrated.

In June of 1933 all political parties except the Nazis were dissolved. A law of July 14 provided for compulsory sterilization of anyone thought to have an hereditary disease, and for children born to liaisons between German women and non-white occupation troops in the Rhineland.

About 300,000 sterilizations were carried out and, as in the case of homosexuals imprisoned (or after 1943 by Himmler's order executed), no compensation, or even suggestion of compensation, seems to have come from Germany to this day.

Skipping a year ahead, during the night of June 30 1934, Hitler directed the murders of the leaders of the SA as well as of several hundred others whom he considered opponents. SA leader Röhm had antagonized the army, the only organization with the power to remove Hitler, by proposing that the 100,000 troops of the Regular Army be integrated into his storm trooper rabble of 2.5 million. The SS was now separated from the SA and under Himmler henceforth pursued a policy of infiltrating the bureaucracy, beginning with the political police, which proved infinitely more succesful than the SA's anarchic attacks from outside. A year and a half of systematic undermining of any sense of legal rectitude in Germany now bore fruit. The bloody purge that shocked the western democracies and finally convinced Hahn that Hitler could not be "reformed," was met from all quarters in Germany with a massive increase in unreserved admiration for the energy, cleverness and courage of the Führer, who had humbled the bullying arrogance of the Party hierarchy and eliminated depraved homosexual elements. In a recent book *(The Hitler Myth)* Ian Kershaw has documented how adoration of the Führer coexisted until the end of the Third Reich with resentment and hatred of the hierarchy and foot-soldiers of the Party.

On August 2 the conservative old elites who had thought to control Hitler lost their last card when, after Hindenburg's death, the office of President was simply merged with that of Chancellor.

My information about the Salem schools in the decade following Meissner's departure in the summer of 1934 comes almost entirely from a memoir written by a surviving staff member in 1949 [26], and in evaluating what is told and what is omitted we should try to take into account the audience that her account was intended for at that time. How did the upper middle class alumni and friends of the school, parents and prospective parents, asses the Third Reich in 1949? Opinion polls taken by occupation forces after the war may give some hazy impression. In 1946 polls showed that one in two Germans thought National Socialism had been a good idea; in 1950 one third still opposed the nearly successful attempt to assassinate Hitler in July 1944, one quarter had a "good opinion" of Hitler, and one tenth thought he was the greatest statesman of the century. According to a poll in the late 1950s, youth believed Hitler had done much good in abolishing unemployment, punishing sexual criminals and introducing cheap radio sets. Many older Germans looking back on the Third Reich today see two strong points: you could leave your bicycle unlocked, and "long-haired layabouts" were hauled off to labor camps. The great change in Hitler's popularity came, of course, only with the "economic miracle" in the1950s, since which approval has been limited to the five to ten percent in the neo-Nazi extreme right. The peoples' goal during the Third Reich was economic recovery; for Hitler this had been only a means to achieve his racial and imperialist goals.

Our chronicler does not venture outside the school precincts, and even within the precincts gives few hints of how and specifically by whom, within the school community, Hitler's goals of territorial expansion and extermination of the Jews were variously perceived. Since events in Germany outside the school are not part of her story, I will try to interpose a few landmarks.

The chronicle reports [26]: "We truly began the summer [of 1934] with the feeling that after the vacation some sort of Hitler Jugend school would replace the old Salem, and no longer considered it possible that the school could retain its old teachers. Although the confidence of parents, students and teachers had vanished, Mittelstrass now wanted to attempt to make Salem viable in the new times by close adherance to the Nazi guidelines. But as if by a miracle no such thing happened." Recognizing the crisis, in October Misterialrat Kraft dismissed Mittelstrass. At this critical point the Director who was henceforth to pilot Salem through the Nazi period was discovered and recruited by the student leaders themselves. The Guardian and others went to nearby Schondorf to call on Heinrich Blendinger, whom they remembered from a talk he had given at Salem, and persuaded him to accept the position. The Ministry was enraged by this development but was overruled when, after long and severe discussion with the student Helpers, Kraft accepted their decision. Kraft had begun to esteem Salem in the time of Meissner; afterwards he became more and more an advocate and protector.

"I will never forget the first assembly that Herr Blendinger convened," the chronicler continues. "He avowed his determination to advance the educational program of Salem and its founder Kurt Hahn with the words: 'Show me the real Salem, as it was meant to be, then I will help you to preserve it.' And now the forces for good were bestirred. Hahn's photograph rested on Herrn Blendinger's desk until a representative of the Ministry personally ordered its removal. He even received permission from the Ministry to to correspond with Herrn Hahn on pedagogic questions."

Aerial view of the Markgraf von Baden's estate that housed the Salem school and (clockwise): Erich Meissner; Heinrich Blendinger with the Markgraf Berthold at a Salem athletic event in the thirties; Kurt Hahn.

"Blendinger followed another road." Contrasting him with Meissner at his eightieth birthday celebration, Hahn thus paid qualified tribute to a different strategy of resistance [10]. "He did not throw the gauntlet to the Nazis; he protected the Salem that had been entrusted to him by the quiet influence of his noble character. Blendinger succeeded in preserving the tranquil rhythym of daily life despite the violent intrusions of the Nazis."

Blendinger shepherded Salem until the last year of the war. The school chronicler summarizes [26] the years 1934-39 as "a time of continuous parrying of open and concealed attacks from many sides. Every few months we were plunged into a danger from outside. Something was always happening that made us suspect to the National Socialist regime, and unfortunately there were always known or anonymous people who hastened to report our 'misdeeds.' One time it was that we had not used the 'Heil Hitler' greeting, another that the chorus had practiced 'Tochter Zion,' or a teacher had said something questionable in class, a student had expressed displeasure over his duties in the Hitler Jugend, or a derogatory comment on the SS or the Führer had been overheard, or then we were supposed to have secretly celebrated Herrn Hahn's birthday—there was always something going on. Again and again the dissolution of the school was threatened, and Herr Blendinger was always busy negotiating reconciliations. Once we were informed unofficially that the decision to close the school had already been taken. Herr Blendinger rushed head over heels to Karlsruhe, where he managed to calm the storm by negotiating with Gauleiter Wagner. Although all this confusion may seldom have come to the attention of the students, the agitation among the teachers was severe."

As parents perceived some reconciliation between school and regime there was a wave of applications for admission at Easter 1935, and for the first time in two years a selection could be made. A graphic picture of the students during these years is rather hard to reconstruct from the generalities of the apologist-chronicler: "Throughout this period we had to make some concessions but they touched only the periphery of our life. We ended each class with the 'Heil Hitler' greeting and carried out the Hitler Jugend activities.The mendacity that had become indispensable outwardly was simply accepted as a neccessary evil by the typical Salem student who remained an upright person. This was our way in a time when coarseness and recklessness prevailed, and our youth in general became appallingly crude and immoral. [But] in retospect it was dangerous that we had stressed student self-government, since the easy successes many had in the Hitler Jugend now made them high-handed. 'Helpers' became too conscious of their competence, and hardly recognized the authority of their teachers. The Colorbearers came to be seen as a privileged class. In deference to the "Führerprinzip" [authoritarian principle] they were no longer self-elected, but had to be appointed by Blendinger. Through the constant defending Salem from attacks they also became too involved in defining its principles, and became confused about rules which can not really be spelled out. When those who had been granted the Training Plan had to grade themselves on such things as "Civil Courage", qualities for which no one can honestly give himself a score of plus or minus, the Training Plan could all too easily lead to self-deception." When Hahn remembered this on his eightieth birthday he had turned it around by crediting Blendinger for emphasizing individual conscience by introducing the category "Courage of One's Convictions" into the Training Plan.

Yes, that gives a keyhole glimpse of some "typical" Salem students. Who were the not so typical, the anonymous ones who "hastened to report our misdeeds," who as Meissner reported began to waiver, hesitated, and eventually broke away? For answer we can only turn to other accounts of German youth and their schools at this time. An alternative youth culture had flourished in Germany since the turn of the century but when Hitler came to power, out of about six million young people who were organized in a plethora of youth groups, only one per cent belonged to the Jungvolk (ages 10 to l4), the Hitler Jugend (14 to 18) and the corresponding Nazi organizations for girls. The per cent of total youth in the Nazi organizations grew in the first year from one to 30 percent, and to 63 percent by 1936 and 82 per cent by 1938. In 1936 the Hitler Jugend was given an official mandate, making it equal to home and school, to educate all German youth physically, intellectually and morally. Some of the moral education was not Nazi brainwashing but rather reinforced stereotypes that were already influential in German culture—the glorification of duty, obedience, physical courage and ruthlessness, and contempt for gentleness, moderation, intellect, sensibility and humanity. Sports, outings, campfires and such were undoubtedly the more widely appreciated attractions. But the incoherence of Nazi ideology also allowed the HJ to attract young people of diverse predilection; they might have a proclivity for example to ideas of national and racial arrogance, to the model of the front-line soldier, or to the supposition of a uniquely profound and valuable 'German' culture, or to a backward-looking agrarian Romanticism along with enthusiasim for modern technology. The paramount problem at Salem, as at other schools, was the exacerbation of normal adolescent rebellion against figures of authority; contempt for teachers and for the life of the intellect were constant refrains with Hitler himself and with the leader of the Hitler

Jugend. A despondent report from the Social Democratic underground to leaders in exile [29] characterizes the allure of the Hitler Jugend even for working-class youth, the least likely to be captivated: "The drill, the uniform, the camp life, the fact that school and the parental home take a back seat—all that is marvelous. Young workers also join in: the national community is better than being the lowest class. That is roughly what they are thinking. The new generation has never had much use for eduation and reading. Now nothing is demanded of them; on the contrary, knowledge is publicly condemned. The young people demand from their parents that they become good Nazis and give up dealing with Jews."

It is somewhat heartening to learn that after 1938 this Nazi youth program began to be repudiated (Detlev Peukert, *Inside Nazi Germany*) precisely by the first generation that had passed its entire youth under totalitarian coercion, though the repudiation mostly took forms closer to delinquency than idealism. Behind the propaganda image German society was, in fact, remarkably disunited through all the years of the Third Reich. It sometimes seems as if the fictitiousness of the Nazi image of a *Volksgemeinschaft*, with every individual fanatically committed to submerging his will in that of the state, has been compensated ever since by the promotion of this fiction as reality in the popular films and books of the victors.

The school chronicler documents diversity also among Hitler's earliest adherents: "It was remarkable that Salem had such persuasive powers that we frequently won friends among the Nazis who were assigned to bring us under control and who instead were drawn to us, although at heart they did not understand Salem. Thus at the start [of Blendinger's administation] we won over to our side two old *Parteigenossen* [old party members, a word now noted regretfully by the dictionary editors as associated irredeemably with the Nazi party] who had been sent to us as teachers, in order partly just to bring our superficial appearance more in conformity, but at the same time also to make us more amenable in spirit to Nazi influence. Yet while Salem retained qualities seductive to others, there was often something sinister to us about the favorable impression that the school was now making. Through all the chaos we could count on the help of Ministerialrat Kraft, who had become a faithful friend of the school. It was also thanks to the intercession of Herrn Kraft that the Hohenfels branch could be reopened under Fräulein Köppen at Easter 1937. As a result of denunciations by one of her colleagues at Spetzgart she had not been allowed to teach, but Hohenfels was in the province of Hohenzollern, not Baden."

A student in 1937 wrote fifty years later [39] of her memorable teacher and mentor, Heinrich Blendinger, and his influence on the children including those who, like herself, were affected by the Nuremberg racial laws. How was Salem dealing with anti-semitism? A month before Blendinger's appointment, the Guardian and several Helpers had had to resign after the Baden Ministry of Culture demanded that student officers be chosen only from boys of pure Aryan descent. The alumni bulletin characterized that ruling as both foolish and damaging to the school's reputation. From this point on the archive falls silent, leaving no record of the reactions of individual staff and students to the impending catastrophe. But excerpts from a letter addressed by Ministerialrat Kraft to Party headquarters in Munich [41] three years later gives some impression of the growing pressures on Salem, and its accomodations to them:

"You have been informed that an 'indefensible state of affairs prevails in Schlosschule Salem.' The basis for this accusation is an allegation that there are two Jews in this private school. It is true that among the 280 Salem students there are two full-blooded Jews. They have nothing to do with the specific educational program which relates to the boarding school, but attend only for the classroom work. Furthermore they have now been at the institution for many years and have given no grounds for expulsion.

"Today and for a number of years the Schlosschule Salem, which was heavily *verjudet* at the time of the Seizure of Power, has conformed to the National Socialist regulations and has not accepted Jewish students or those of mixed ancestry." The Ministerialrat here cites relevant decrees, beginning with the "Statute on the Overcrowding of German Schools" of April 25th 1933. "In order, however, to purify the Salem school completely of Jews I have, on October 21st 1935, established the following guidelines: from today on non-Aryan students will no longer be admitted; those non-Aryan students already enrolled may not, from this day on, be invested with any office in the classroom or the school. With regard to exchange students from abroad, non-Aryans are not welcome—this applies also to so-called emigrants, even if Aryan, who are for example enrolled in Hahn's new establishment in England. If today there are still two Jews in the institution, this is only due to the circumstance that they were already enrolled before the Seizure of Power. Since both are expected to leave the school at the end of this year, there will be no more Jewish students after Easter 1938.

"Soon after he Seizure of Power on January 30, 1933 I was summoned to Berlin and advised on behalf of Minister Frick that the Salem school was to be preserved so far as possible." (A colorless bureaucrat who implemented many of Hitler's domestic plans, Wilhelm Frick was convicted by the Nuremberg Tribunal, and hanged). "I have tried to fully adhere to these directions and have attempted to bring this school, which is renowned throughout he world, into conformity with the National Socialist spirit. This was not a simple task and could not be done in a day. To persuade him to accept my demands I had even at one time to threaten the Markgraf von Baden, the landlord and head of the boarding school, with being taken into protective custody. Today one can assert unequivocally that the school is guided and led in the National Socialist spirit. In recent years it has achieved outstanding success in the field of International athletic competitions. I am remembering that for three succesive years it has triumphed in the English field and track competitions. The team was even received by the King of England and invited to tea. If this school were now to be destroyed, as [your correspondent] wishes, Germany's enemies throughout the world would rejoice. I also call attention to the fact that a nephew of the Führer's Deputy [Rudolf Hess] has been at the school for the past two years and is an enthusiastic partisan. I understand that your correspondents want to employ every means to destroy the school. I would be grateful if you would inform them that they are henceforth not to undertake any more disrupting attacks."

Kraft disapeared after the war, and various stories circulated—that, remorseful, he had committed suicide, or had even been originally dispatched by the Social Democrats to pose as a faithful Party member.

It is fair to assume that many staff and students were horrified by this racial accommodation to the Nazis. However, some were not. Remarkable as it sounds, the Jewish Question seems to have been of no more than minimal interest to most Germans through all the years culminating in the Holocaust. Hitler's belief that shared hatred of the Jews would cement the unity of the Reich and propitiate the conquered peoples of Europe was in vain. A boycott of Jewish businesses, doctors and lawyers proclaimed in April 1933 had to be canceled after only a single day, and for some years thereafter Hitler took pains to dissociate his public image from the seamier sides of anti-semitism. The justification he gave the Reichstag for supporting the anti-Jewish Nuremberg Laws in 1935 was that they would head off spontaneous "defensive actions by the enraged population." Unfortunately many non-Aryans were deceived by his assurance that the laws, denying citizensip and banning marriage and sexual relations between Jews and "Aryans," would replace acts of random harassment with the possibility of peaceful separate existence. Hitler again tested the waters in November 1938 with a quasi-medieval night of organized terror by the Party and the SA, the *Reichskristallnacht.* This was the only occasion in the twelve years of the Third Reich that the German people were directly confronted with the full savagery behind Hitler's intentions, and the population met it with nearly universal disapproval.

Where the Nazis succeeded was in depersonalizing Jews in Germany using forced emigration, concentration in big city ghettos in 1939, and the compulsory yellow star in 1941. With their progressive isolation from society "Jews" became something abstract. During the war Hitler reversed his public image as he became anxious to be personally associated with the Holocaust and make his work manifest in the eyes of history. Apathy supplemented the widespread passive anti-semitism in Germany in the war years, and terror was rarely needed to enforce silence about the final solution. With the precedents of the massacre of Soviet war prisoners by the Wehrmacht and of Soviet Jews by the Einsatzgruppen, the murder of six million Jews may have aquired some aura of inevitability to the administrators of the Polish camps.

Salem was not a denominational school but Protestant services and religious holidays, which my diary shows had figured large in school life, soon also came under attack, as reported by the chronicler: "The prescribed 'National' holidays were also observed, but our hearts were not in them. Our hearts were with the old festivals, our Sunday chapel music, our concerts, our productions of classical plays, our Adventszeit with its special enchantment, our Christmas play, which indeed we were able to preserve until 1938. The 'Cultural Director' assigned to us, whose decision about the Christmas play was decisive, told us that the play had much force, but a force that was not Nazi, and that it therefore could not be performed again. He was much impressed by the demeanour of the children at a rehearsal, which he attended unrecognized and without our knowledge; he recognized the artistic and ethical value of the play, but it was ideologically unacceptable. None of us who experienced the last Christmas play will ever forget it. In the following years we sought a substitute in lovely musical performances, in 1939 with excerpts of Handel's Messiah, with its final gorious Hallelujah. This provoked a collision with the SS Regimental Medical Officer who was with us as director of the future military hospital, who complained that young German men should be singing Hallelujah."

For a few months at the start of the war the school occupied the Markgraf's estate only under a pledge to evacuate to a distant hotel on two hours notice, until tentative plans for conversion to a military hospital were abandoned. A physician, who had nothing to do with the school, took it on himself to prohibit the singing of the Messiah! It seems now an appropriate moment for another look at the respectable middle class whose anti-semitism was only passive, who were shocked by the Kristallnacht pogrom and deplored this public violence by the uneducated hoodlums in the SA. It was not hoodlums who administered the Holocaust. Doctors and lawyers, the premier affluent professionals in contemporary society, were grossly overrepresented in the Nazi Party leadership even before the Seizure of Power. Later, one in ten in the leadership corps of the SS had studied law, and similar numbers of "promising" young lawyers were found among the administrators of the death camps and of the Einsatz groups who followed the Wehrmacht through Poland and massacred Jews and Soviet Kommissars.

But let's look more closely at the doctor who prohibited the Messiah. He was an SS Regimental officer. Policy enforced from Berlin was that all killing at Auschwitz and other camps was to be done exclusively by such SS doctors who were assigned to the camps—the selection of those to be killed, the supervision of the gassing, and the confirmation of its success. Refusal of this assignment was considered desertion. It was widely understood that any doctor could accept transfer to the eastern front as an alternative, but there is no record that any ever did so. Robert Jay Lifton in *The Nazi Doctors* has meticulously documented through interviews with many of these doctors after the war that they were of diverse personality types and backgrounds and had chosen the healing profession for conventional reasons. Polish and Jewish prisoner doctors who were allowed to live were drawn into the killing operations, and into collaborating with the less well trained SS doctors in their crudely conceived and sadistic experiments on prisoners. Lifton concludes: "No individual self is inherently evil, murderous, genocidal. Yet under certain conditions virtually any self is capable of becoming all of these," and he has written what is for me the most terrifying of all accounts of the Holocaust.

Hitler's only resounding domestic defeats were at the hands of the organized Christian churches. First, in 1934 he attempted to replace the Protestant hierarchy with Reichs Bishops who repudiated the Old Testament and its Jewish morality and some of whom associated Christian Communion with Jewish ritual slaughter. Defeat came again in 1941 when he was forced to terminate the secret euthanasia of mentally or physically handicapped Germans after it was denounced from the pulpit by Catholic Bishop Galen of Münster. But, as confirmed by the cited incidents at Salem, in 1935-38 the Nazis successfully overcame church opposition to their control of the schools. Resignation, indifference, apathy, fear bore fruit as denominational public schools were replaced by "community" schools, crucifixes and religious pictures were forcibly removed, pastors arrested and nuns dismissed from teaching posts. It is often asked why the churches, which alone had the cohesion to resist the Nazis, were silent about civil rights, infringement of personal liberties (except those of priests) and policies of racial hatred. Had they the inclination to resist these abuses, which seems to have been the case only among a minority of the hierarchy, their silence before the Nazis came to power would have limited their options later.

Bishop Galen's sermon that ended the euthanasia of handicapped ethnic Germans proved also to be only a pyrrhic victory. The cyanide killing facilities in psychiatric and other hospitals continued to be used during the period of transition to the large scale killing camps (Robert J. Lifton, *The Nazi Doctors*). Even in early 1941 psychiatrists were sent to the concentration camps to select "asocial elements" for transfer to their hospitals. Later selections for transport were made directly by the camp SS doctors, Jew becoming a "collective diagnosis" for asocial element, apparently without any objection from the hospital psychiatrists. About 20,000 victims perished in the German hospitals. During a brief transition while the hospital cyanide facilities were being copied on a large scale at Auschwitz, phenol injection into the heart was substituted so that killing need not take place on German soil.

At Salem the chronicler does not specify interference during this time in the content of classroom instruction, less accessible to intruders than theatre and musical performance. History, biology and literature were the major Nazi targets, but a sample exam question at the time of the euthanasia program shows that even Math was not exempt [29]: "There are 300,000 mentally ill. How much do these people cost, at four marks per head (per day)? How many houses at 15,000 marks each could have been built each year for that amount?"

The nationalist bias of history teachers, evident from my diary, was now reinforced by guidelines such as [29]: "The German nation in its essence is the subject of the teaching of history. The certainty of a great national existence is for us based on recognition of the racial forces of the German nation ... the powerless and insignificant have no history." Still I am sure Salem never followed the injunction to make *Mein Kampf* "our infallible pedagogical guiding star," or promoted in biology courses the selection of racially sound marriage partners and the sterilization of inferiors.

Wartime dominated the second half of Blendinger's administration, from 1939 to 1943. The capitulation of France, which brought the "Hitler myth" to its zenith in June 1940, was the only time in the Third Reich when a popular "war mood" comparable to that of 1914 prevailed.

Daily life continued much as normal, many skilled workers and farmers were exempted from military service, and there was no serious rationing of consumer goods. Hitler's fear of working class revolt precluded the measures to enforce domestic austerity that prevailed in England and, later, in America. Peukert (*Inside Nazi Germany*) has calculated that Nazi Germany actually did not rearm to more than half strength until 1943. The fall of France also cost Salem its ace in the hole, as hysterical anti-British hate propaganda replaced the lingering hope for some reconciliation with the Aryan cousins. "It was indeed remarkable that so far, although Salem had been much threatened, little had actually been done. In the early years we had the feeling that Salem was being protected for political reasons in deference to a possible English alliance. 'What can you do against Salem,' exclaimed Robert Ley in a rage, 'when the King of England welcomes Salemers.' This was after the third victory of the Salem field and track team, competing in London against the teams from 120 English boarding schools." Ley, an alcoholic chemist who became Minister of Labor, hanged himself in his prison cell before he could be sentenced at the Nuremberg trials. "But during the war this rationale evaporated, and the Party was encouraged to take complete charge of the rearing of children and to close down all private schools." Pressures on private schools took such forms as loss of tax concessions, rigged local plebiscites and regulations forbidding civil servants and the military from enrolling their children.

The chronicler continues: "Still we hoped with our innate optimism that we might even now retain an exceptional position. A visit from Reichminister Rust in November 1941 encouraged this optimism." A friend of Hitler since the twenties, Rust had boasted after his appointment as Reich Minister of Education that he had "liquidated the school as an institution of intellectual acrobatics" overnight. "He spoke to be sure of accentuating the Nazi character of youth education, but he wanted also to protect the inherant nature of Salem; he proposed to put Salem directly under the supervision of the German Minister of Education. By this arrangement we would have come under the centralized control of the Reich, that is of the Party, while the Province of Baden would have born the financial responsibility. That was probably the reason that the provincial goverment was not very interested. Again and again a deadline was announced for the state to take over, only for it to expire unheralded. The Markgraf, and all of us along with him, still hoped that the negotiations could be drawn out until the awaited collapse of the Nazi regime, in which we firmly believed. This hope was fulfilled! Salem was never taken over by the state! Never the less after August 1941 the school association and the Markgraf had little control, either on life at the school or on the composition of the teaching staff, since after that all residential schools including those that were not state property were subject to supervision by the national boarding school office.

"As the war progressed there were more and more far-reaching consequences for the school. The proportion of Juniors and girls increased. Classroom instruction was circumscribed by farm work duty. In the fall of 1942 young teenagers were enlisted into anti-aircraft units, so that now the intermediate classes were also affected. Along with this came a terrifying instability, since some of them were much too young to be trusted on their own. Teachers took turns every two weeks to visit and supervise these auxiliaries. With the increasing frequency of alerts control became impossible." These fifteen-and sixteen-year olds called up to help man anti-aircraft batteries had been children at the time of Hitlers "triumphs;" now the image of the Führer as military genius was fading in a hail of bombs. Area bombing, which eventually damaged a quarter of the homes in Germany, caused the death of over 300,000 and evacuation of five million, left the region around the Salem schools untouched. Though it did nothing to promote military victory, it did depress morale and channel hatred against the Nazi regime for its failure to ward off the attacks.

"After August 1941 our supervison was under the direction of SS Obergruppenführer Heissmeyer. The first alarm was a twelve day investigation by SS Sturmbahnführer Pein, prompted by a very incriminating phone call from a recently enrolled student who was a nephew of Reichsleiter Bouhler, about criticisms of the SS and the Führer by fellow students. But we were protected by the magic charm of Salem. Herr Pein required the dismissal of the most highly incriminated students, but chose the role of protector of Salem, even though we were worlds apart. SS-Führers came more and more frequently to inspect us. They were never satisfied, constantly calling for reforms, but nothing happened. Even a visit from Heissmeyer himself produced no decisive change. He showed no interest whatever in the spiritual life of the school; only superficial appearances were reviewed and judged.

"But then something took place which was a great misfortune for Salem. In the Spring of 1943 Herr Blendinger became seriously ill, so ill that after a few months it became clear that it was out of the question for him to resume the direction of the school. Nothing worse could have happened, for now it was revealed that it was only the conciliatory personality of Herr Blendinger that had been able to keep either the teaching staff or the Helpers united. Each now took a different view of the Principles of Salem. Every discussion on this question was fruitless, since we simply no longer understood each other. Mistrust and misunderstandings led to wrangling which could not be kept hidden. Clearly the staff was split in two and the rupture was unhealable."

The author of this account has not chosen, writing only four years after the war, to further identify the two incompatible factions, beyond hints along the way that younger teachers had joined the SA "in the interests of the school," and were then made probational Party members, and others had joined the Nazi Teacher's League (NSLB) but "attended meetings infrequently." One can only invoke general accounts of teachers of the Third Reich to guess at possible attributes of this faceless faction. Like doctors and lawyers, teachers swarmed into the Party in the first year. By the end of 1933 twenty five per cent were members, as opposed to five percent of the general population, and by 1937 ninety seven per cent belonged to the NSLB, whose main functions were ideological indoctrination of its members, and vetting them for promotion on the basis of political reliability. A fervent belief in the "ideals" of Naziism is suggested by the fact that they formed an an extraordinarilly high proportion of minor Party functionaries. Party work rested overwhelmingly on their shoulders in the countryside, where they were often seen as adversaries of the local clergy. Even though their profession was subject to contemptuous villification by Nazi leaders and constant interferance by the Hitler Jugend, they apear to have remained more ideologically motivated than any other group. Kershaw in *Popular Opinion and Political Dissent in the Third Reich* quotes An NSLB report in 1938 stressing that teachers, like other "civil servants, were the citizens who most sincerely approved of the Third Reich. There was probably not one who did not rejoice at the creation of Greater Germany. The persecution of the Jews was almost generally understood and welcome. Only a few old bureaucrats regretted the measures taken in November [the Kristallnacht pogrom]." The last statement may have exaggerated to ingratiate, as the report was a plea for higher pay for teachers. Teachers at a private school were not civil servants, and we can never know to what extent a few staff at Salem may have been attuned to such sentiments of their colleagues elsewhere.

But now the chronicle of Salem's last year and a half under the Third Reich will illuminate all too clearly the kinds of things it had hitherto fought against becoming. At the end of 1943 Blendinger, who had earlier suffered a severe stroke, addressed this farewell note to the school [42]:

"This common letter must stand in for many individual ones, as writing is still difficult for me. I am delighted by every letter I get from you; don't hold it against me if I answer so little.

"The most important thing that I have to tell you about Salem is that, for the duration of my illness, Obergruppenführer Heissmeyer has appointed as acting Director Dr. Schmitt. Accordingly for the first time decisions about the school direction will be taken out of our hands, and it is of course possible that some of the Salem ways will be changed. But we have a firm belief in the inner strength of Salem, and Obergruppenführer Heissmayer as well as Dr. Schmitt should take note that a worthy spirit reigns at Salem, which is worth preserving. Be faithful to Salem and preserve your loyalty to us outwardly and inwardly!

"Today on the first day of the year 1944 I want to send you also some words of Rilke, that he wrote some time ago to a friend at New Year, and that have a special significance for the year ahead: 'We want to believe that it will be a long year that is granted us, fresh, untouched, full of things that never were before, of work never done before, of tasks, claims, exacting demands. We want to see that we shall learn to accept it without letting overmuch slip past us of that which it can bestow on those who long for all that is indispensable, solemn and immense.'" I hope this rash attempt to translate the great poet is not totally garbled.

The Chronicle continues: "The new year brought a solution to the conflict in a form which had been long feared: we learned at the beginning of January 1944 that the Inspectorate of Heimschulen had confirmed the appointment of SS Obersturmführer Dr. Schmitt as director. And a few days later the SS man took charge. With marked politeness he presented himself as a good Santa Claus, who distributes his gifts or threatens with the switch as needed. Salem was to become an earthly paradise for students and teachers. He could provide everything—foodstuffs, missing household utensils, servants, above all a fabulous cook, who would prepare mayonnaise and other splendors for the staff. Thank god we never saw anything of all these splendors, and our good Fräulein Anna cooked on until April 1st 1945, when she was pensioned by the school after 25 years of service. The number of teachers was to be increased; by incorporation into the civil service our lives were to be 'secured.' Our meeting room was to be transformed for ceremonial purposes and the dining hall consecrated by decoration with National Socialist colors. And after the war a splendid new structure would be erected on the old heap with every conceivable luxury! We did not see much of all these great changes. Elaborately inscribed maxims appeared in the hallways and stairwells, and indeed large pictures of our 'Führer' were hung in long rows for the first time in the dining hall. Students were required to memorize the names and titles of the leaders, and often after meals one was summoned to rattle them off, but he usually got stuck, especially when there was a higher-up visting. Before lunch one of the boys in HJ uniform, supported by a second, would say some snappy words, which everyone present would repeat, and after lunch we sang a song of the Movement, which often sounded cheerless and had to be repeated with louder volume."

Some flavor of such snappy words may be given by the vow taken on admission to the Jungvolk:

"You, Führer, are our commander!
We stand in your name.
The Reich is the object of our struggle,
It is the beginning and the Amen."

Though I don't remember the Hitler salute as my brother and Prince Phillip do at Spetzgart, the alternating hysterical screams and stolid beats of the "Horst Wessel" song of the Movement ring in my ears to this day.

"In the dining hall Herr Schmitt would hold forth to deliver a dressing down or provide military and political sermons. The flag muster on Monday mornings provided an occasion for the most intrepid predictions of the coming victory. Classes became squads and teachers were promoted to be squad leaders. We were able to help some students to hold fast. Even the color-bearer meetings could be continued but Herrn Schmitt and the Nazi teachers exploited these student officers for their own purposes, so that they became tools in their hands under the deceptive appearance of preserving the old spirit of Salem. To add to the disorder another Nazi teacher appeared in March 1944, Herr Dr. Kötke (though not in SS-uniform), who was also commissioned by the Boarding School Inspectorate with the title of Director. Apparently there had been a split into two camps within the Inspectorate, one of whom had sent us Herrn Schmitt, the other Herrn Klötke as replacement or counterbalance to Herrn Schmitt."

This episode of the rival Directors provides a peephole through which one can note another instance where the Nazi propaganda image of Germany seems to have triumphed over the reality in later popular acounts (from the victors camp) describing a powerful monolithic administration. Kershaw (*The Nazi Dictatorship*) has characterized the internal administration of the Third Reich as the disintegration of central government into chaos, as Hitler's predisposition to let rivals fight it out, and then side with the winner, led to the dissolution of government into a multiplicity of competing and non-coordinated ministries and party offices.

As 1944 unfolded, great events passed uncommemorated by the Salem chronicler. On June 6 the Anglo-American landing in Normandy, and on July 20 the famous, nearly succesful assassination attempt, when an English-made bomb concealed in Colonel von Stauffenberg's briefcase detonated during Hitler's daily war conference. One of the key organizers of this assassination attempt, and a member of the immediate circle around Stauffenberg, was in the senior class that graduated from Spetzgart just as I arrived [the photograph on page 80 shows him with a group of classmates who have just taken the final math exam]. In Gestapo custody on July 21st, he took his own life to avoid the possibility of betraying his comrades under torture.

Salem does not emphasize any list of alumni who participated in the "resistance," a capacious word which accommodates a variety of claimants. There had been many assassinations planned before the final near success of July 20. A participant in one of them, Axel von der Bussche, though not an alumnus, served as Director of Salem from 1959 to 1961. A student at that time recalls [43] that on the fifteenth anniversary of the July attempt he held a school assembly under the "Polish Linden tree." Near the end of the war two Polish forced laborers had been hanged from this tree, just outside the Salem grounds. They were alleged to have had intercourse with German women. The student remembers that "at this assembly we students first came to understand Axel von der Bussche as a resistance fighter." Along with a later President of Germany, Richard von Weizsäcker, he had been an officer in a Prussian infantry regiment that lost eighteen officers in the resistance against National Socialism. In the autumn of 1942 the 24-year-old officer had witnessed the systematic massacre of Jews near Dudno in the Ukraine [43]. "Eight hundred Jewish men, women and children stood there in the November sun waiting to be stacked head to foot like herring in a mass grave and killed by a shot in the neck. Nothing like this had ever been seen in the so-called western world. What was happening here was the most significant event of the century—organized mass murder, ordered by a head of state." A year later came the opportunity to participate in one of von Stauffenberg's assassination plans, when he was sent to Berlin with a regimental detachment that was to exhibit the new winter uniforms to the Führer. The plan was to conceal, in a pocket of the knapsack he would carry, a bomb that would be detonated during the demonstration. At the same moment he would throw himself on Hitler. But, as so often, Providence intervened: during the preceding night a train containing the whole collection of winter gear was destroyed by English bombardment. A year later the same bomb, safely preserved in his knapsack for another opportunity, was under the hospital bed where he was confined after losing a leg in combat, when the Gestapo came to interrogate him on July 21.

Hahn was among those people of good will who repudiated assassination attempts out of hand. In any case coups d'etat on these lines were options open only to the military. The British have been criticized for turning a deaf ear to overtures from the German military resistance, and limiting their war time propaganda to attempts to alienate the working class. Such propaganda may have been idle yet, in a broad sense, it seems now agreed that resistance by workers formed by far the most effective component of the German resistance movement. It was from fear of labor unrest that until 1943 wartime mobilization had reached only half its maximum potential.

The Chronicle resumes at the end of 1944: "The enemy advance into Alsace and the decision of our leaders to forcibly enlist the German people in a final battle was destined to finish the transformation of Salem. It was to be made into a battleground for the Nazi regime, a fortress. By October the Hohenfels and Hermannsberg branches had been expropriated by the Armed Forces, and in December 1944 we were all dismissed. Frau Kupffer holed up at Hermannsberg and Fräulein Köppen at Hohenfels to bide their time, as Fräulein Ewald had done ever since 1933 in her retreat at Salem. Our places were now taken by Nazi teachers, most of whom were refugees from Alsace. Entire classes were taken in with their teachers from other schools at Napola Rufach and elsewhere, and they brought with them carloads of goods of dubious origin. Some of our old students departed, but most did not know where to turn because their homes no longer existed."

Not content with transforming existing schools, the Nazis created several new school systems intended to produce an elite for the regime. The *Napolas* were boarding schools under SS influence modelled on former Prussian military cadet schools. In the Adolf Hitler schools and *Ordensburgen* Nazi colleges, run by the Hitler Jugend entirely outside the state school system, indoctrination replaced education so completely that entrants were recruited with difficulty. At the University level the secret "German Student League", limited to less than five per cent of all students and characterized by Führer's Deputy Hess as "a sort of intellectual SS," was to provide training for future high functionaries, especially for the SD or secret Security Service.

"As the military catastrophe unfolded unmistakably, the control of Salem shifted on April 1st to a former district leader from Alsace. His furniture and luggage had barely arrived in the hallways of the school when the remainder of our armed forces poured through in full retreat, and the higher ranks bivouaced overnight in the school buildings leaving everything in appalling disorder. Herr Schmitt brought the remaining Spetzgart girls and female staff to Salem.

"On April 21 sirens sounded the long alarm indicating the imminent breakthrough of the enemy tanks." This occasioned the new director together with the older boys—so far as they followed him—to take flight to the Allgäu, to "escape the clutches of the enemy." Meantime the preceding director, Herr Schmitt, prepared to defend Salem with the students, SS-personnel and members of the armed forces who sided with him. Since he was amply supplied with hand grenades and anti-tank and machine gun ammunition, our situation was quite hazardous. We had a hunch that he himself—his wife and son had been sent off by car the moment the alarm sounded—would disappear by similar transport when the right moment came, but we were obliged to anticipate that he would first, by reckless attack on enemy tanks, sacrifice Salem to bombardment. Thank God the French forces delayed occupying Salem, while all the villages around us were taken one by one, so that the position became uncomfortable for Herr Schmitt, faced with the danger that he might be deprived of a timely excuse for taking flight, and early one morning we found that he and his entourage had disappeared. Then the occupation by the French forces proceeded without difficulties.

"Since after April 1st all the children had departed who were able to go back to relatives, at this time only about sixty remained. The Markgraf viewed it as of the utmost importance that the Nazi Schule Salem be completely shut down and dissolved. Accordingly the last boys and girls were lodged with farmers, or sent to the Hermannsberg where they could work as apprentices in the workshop. From July to November 1945 Schule Schloss Salem ceased to exist. The Nazi teachers also disappeared more or less promptly, some only after extensive interrogation by the French."

On November 12 the Markgraf addressed [3] 20 boarders and about 80 day students and the reassembled old staff at the reopening of Schule Schloss Salem: "Today a youth which has been abused, uprooted and deceived returns and has no home," he said, in part. "On the pretext that they must become 'tough,' they have become systematically anaesthetized to the suffering of humanity. Slander and persecution of others is now part of their daily perception of life. Through glorification of themselves they became detached from the authority of elders and teachers, and the basest potentialities were unleashed by enjoined denunciations, that did not even stop at family members. A responsible teacher might well be deterred from attempting to correct these incalculable ravages. During the war hundreds of thousands were seized by a passionate determination to exterminate. In our children a passion must be ignited to help those in distress and poverty. Parents entrust to us the most priceless thing they possess. The task now is to prepare children, coming from a world of wreckage, for a new life."

CHAPTER 8

Salem Accommodates and Thrives: 1945-1995

"Salem sparkles in times when courage is lacking in a dispirited educational establishment. Out of the discarded stage props of the student revolt and the residue of tradition Salem has clobbered together an historic compromise. Despite uncertainty about the right path, the school radiates self-confidence verging on self-satisfaction." As this account from *Die Zeit* (29 Nov. 1985) implies, a visitor today would find some Hahnian features missing: the uniform, the Training Plan (except in the junior school at Hohenfels), the Colorbearers acting as ministers without portfolio.

Of the five hundred students at Salem today fifteen percent are of foreign origin and one fourth receive some financial aid. The Hermannsberg branch, where Hahn settled for his last years, was sold after his death in 1974. Ages ten to twelve are at Hohenfels, thirteen to seventeen at Salem, and eighteen to nineteen are in a distinct and more collegiate program at Spetzgart, modeled somewhat on the United World Colleges. Each year about two dozen students from the Middle School spend at least one term in one of the twenty affiliated schools around the world, and there is also a faculty exchange. Salem is portrayed in the German media as the most renowned school in Germany; it attracts more applicants with each passing year, yet a poll of parents in the surrounding areas showed a consensus that they would not choose to send their children to this school for bigwigs, and they attributed ignoble motives to parents who did so.

Fraulein Ewald, who had spent the Nazi period in seclusion, occupying herself by cataloging local wildflowers of the Salem valley, returned as Director for three years after the war. Foreign and working-class students were absent during these years when outside financial assistance made it possible to enroll many refugees as well as children from military circles involved in the resistance. In the disorder following the war Hahn found that there was a spiritual vacuum in young people, yet he felt they were ready for a new inspiration and even longing for it. At the same time the persistent badgering by the military occupation forces in favor of "re-education" along foreign models was an inadequate solution. "Re-education is the wrong word; restoration is the proper term." But by 1950 he still saw [20] German youth as "an immense crowd of self-seekers, without faith or standards and lacking all public spirit."

The decade of the fifties, during which the school was directed by the Prince of Hanover (a student in my time who was later, like the Markgraf Berthold, to be married to one of Prince Phillip's four sisters), brought first the economic miracle, a sudden unforseen prosperity stimulated by the American policy of strengthening Germany against the Soviets, and then a wave of student unrest and revolt. Hahn condemned the consumerism that accompanied the economic miracle (a sentiment hardly shared by the profane masses) and, even blamed [10] the big city milieu and obsessions with sex, science and technology. He saw the ground gained in one term being lost during the vacation to coddling and unruliness.

Student unrest, which came on the heels of miraculous prosperity, began in the universities. Although four thousand university teachers had lost their jobs in 1945 because of their open avowal of Nazi principles (as against only seventeen hundred initially discharged by the Nazis in 1933), the rigidly hierarchical faculties had retained their traditional conservative conformist tradition.The students demanded participation in decision-making, beginning in 1960. These demands, although resisted, did influence reforms in the teaching of German history (which, since the war, had tended to come as far as Bismarck and then stop abruptly in confusion): the distortions of the Weimar texts were replaced by segments on the Nazi period and the holocaust. With stonewalling by the university hierarchies, and as student population tripled to 900,000 creating a volatile academic proletariat with diminished job prospects in teaching and the civil service, the student movement was taken over by extremists. An anarchist subculture, echoing the age-old German romantic contempt for reason, spread havoc in the universities and culminated in the affluent leftist terrorists of the seventies.

What trickled down from universities to Salem and other secondary schools was largely hedonism, drinking and marijuana, demands for sexual freedom, and the goal (as a Salem student newsletter put it) of instilling fear and trembling in the classroom teacher. In the view of at least some friends of Salem who had lived through both, its principles suffered more severely during the period from 1960 to 1974 than they had during the Third Reich.

There was a period of musical chairs in the directorship, and public service projects were emphasized to counteract chaos, particularly projects involving the dispatching of student teams to disasters in far away places: Greece, Florence, Brittany, southern Italy. Community Service projects cited in a recent catalogue include tending to the old and infirm, brigades dedicated to fire, water or accident rescue, and a construction crew for emergency building, bridge and road repair, as well as "green" projects such as supervising recycling centers and building nesting boxes for endangered birds. Over the years some of the specific practices Salem had employed to embody its ideals were abandoned, often after a transiently observed veto by Hahn. It is not clear what if anything has taken their place to promote the goals of self-knowledge and self-discipline, of concern for others, and of education for responsibility. The time when it seemed an honor to be a colorbearer, or just to be at Salem at all, seems long past.

Alumni recalling Hahn's visits during these years [9] speak of a haggard worthy old man with a big hat, whose ideals belonged to a time long past, an obsolete ineffective old man who could not understand them and who did not want to see what was happening around him.

The self-graded Training Plan which served Hahn's categoric imperative of self-knowledge and self-disciplne survived at Gordonstoun. An English teacher who knew both schools explained it this way [44]: "The system of trust alone would be of no value. It would be like the center pole of a tent, which gives a false sense of security when it is not abetted by tent pegs around the periphery. English Public School traditions made it easier to multiply the number of pegs and to find people to hammer them properly into place."

"Salem had to change to have continuity" wrote an alumnus in 1986 [39], citing the theme of a recent alumni reunion, Education for Responsibility in a Democracy. "Students are no longer appointed to responsible positions," the alumnus continued, "but are elected. Democracy requires independence of heart and mind, civil courage, a sense of proportion and talent for conflict resolution. All these virtues must be cultivated from an early age. By [practice in self-government] students learn about the power of groups, about minorities and majorities, they encounter indifference and fervour, learn about the manipulability of individuals and groups, and that good nature can be abused and craftiness can succeed. And they can realize that one is not helpless but can learn to ride out conflicts and win acceptance for what one recognizes as right." An admirable response to the heritage of the Third Reich, the failed Weimar Republic, and the autocracy of Bismarck and the Wilhelmine period. Yet one could hardly expect elected officers to perpetuate the Salem traditions served by the Helpers and Colorbearers in Hahn's time.

This emphasis on Democracy is at the root of a long-standing and tedious conflict with the current Markgraf Max, grandson and namesake of the founder, which has mushroomed into a crisis in the nineties. This grandson had been enrolled in Gordonstoun in 1946, which he seems not to have cared for. Before his death in 1963, his father had changed the school charter so that Markgraf Max, although landlord of the Salem branch, would henceforth be only one voice among several in its administration. This voice was soon sharply raised when two young unmarried teachers became pregnant. He proposed that they be discharged, but no one listened to him. Other disputes simmered until, at a press conference in February 1989, he announced that he considered the present Salem lax, dissolute and liberal; he would not renew the school's lease when it terminated in 1999, and that moreover he intended at that time to found a rival "Schule Salem" at his estate. Some of his further comments may sketch his irrascible personality. He remarked [45] that "my own children attended the school, at least for a time. They very soon became Room Captains. Democracy was practiced to the letter, when the children had no comprehension of Democracy. That meant the children who sought out the office always got elected. And the others went along as passive passengers. After a while the officers said, why should we take the responsiblity when others don't? Then they resigned their appointments...In the old days the names were printed on the school uniforms. You could tell who was wearing someone else's clothes without permission. When I suggest school uniforms, the others answer: black pants, brown shirts, shoulder straps, regular Hitler Jugend. These teachers think they are very clever, and they weren't old enough even to make a mess in their pants in the days of the Hitler Jugend." In his redneck fashion the Markgraf has touched on the problem of "fascistoid" human practices and qualities, things which had been considered virtues for a long time, perhaps for millenia, but which having been espoused by the Nazis are liable to be questioned or even repudiated now, and for some time to come. It seems quite understandable that this time might be rather longer in Germany than elsewhere.

The following month Dr. Bueb, the Director since 1974, countered to eight hundred alumni gathered in his support; he defended himself as "through and through conservative," but added that "conservative education today can't consist only of drill and cold showers. Young people can not be treated today as they were then, whether one thinks this would be desirable or not."

The author and Jocelin Winthrop Young at Spetzgart, and the eighteenth century Salem gatehouse, in 1991. The Spetzgart harbor in 1933 and today; the boy with the hat and the unmistakably American style with the hammer is Dennis.

Now, hoping to turn adversity to advantage, the school proposes to try to build a new campus, an international college, in a new location for the Upper School, and to offer as an alternative to the Abitur exam the International Baccalaureate degree which is presently accepted in sixty two other countries but has been adamantly rejected in Germany. Instruction will be in English, the "extended essay" of the IB will be required, and evening seminars in economics, law, medicine and business are planned through the nearby University in Konstanz.

The past is not forgotten even in times of anxiety for the future. A paragraph in the *New York Times* for October 25, 1992 reported that during the preceeding night in the small town of Überlingen vandals had smashed fifty gravestones in a cemetary for former slave laborers and had daubed swastikas on a plaque memorializing those who had died in the local annex of the Dachau concentration camp. (Today there are only 40,000 Jews in Germany—mostly descendents of *Ostjuden* camp survivors, rather than of the 400,000 Jewish German nationals of 1933). Meantime hostels for foreigners seeking asylum had elsewhere been a target of almost nightly attacks by neo-Nazi gangs, more than 2000 in 1992.

A school bulletin [46] reports that on November 7th students, teachers and Mentors participated in a demonstration against hostility to foreigners organized by the Überlingen gymnasiumn. According to the student reporter: "Twelve hundred participants assembled first in front of what is today the Überlingen hospital, on whose grounds the barracks of the concentration camp had stood. The Überlingen camp was an offshoot of Dachau. In this camp eight hundred people were detained under degrading conditions, obliged to march twice a day, silently and in formation, to a cliff near Überlingen, where their job was to excavate an underground storage place for explosives. The demonstrators followed the same path and assembled again at a memorial plaque at the entrance to the tunnel.

"Two days later on November 9th, the 54th anniversary of the so-called Reichskristallnacht, an evening assembly at Salem took up the theme of 'hostility to foreigners.' After several informative talks students and teachers adjourned to the so-called Polenlinde (Polish lime tree), where during the war two Poles were hanged by the Nazis, for a short talk in memory of this crime. In the face of events in Germany such a gathering can have only modest effects. We must accordingly, right here in Salem, come to grips much more energetically with these menaces."

What is Salem like today? A recent brochure lists some extracurricular offerings. Arts: painting, stage settings, photography; chorus and orchestra, all instruments, concerts, musicals; annual Poet Laureate competition; theatrical productions of Shakespeare, Lessing, Schiller, as well as of contemporary and foreign language plays. Crafts: pottery, cabinet making, metalsmith shop, machine tools, auto repair, gardening, printing, cooking, model building, dressmaking. Sports and games: hockey, basketball, handball, field and track, gym, swimming, dance and jazz gymnastics, tennis, sailing, and wind-surfing as well as other team sports.

But such a brochure, of course, epitomizes one of the countless contemporary genres of promotional writing. So what is it really like to be a student at Salem? Here are a few scattered student voices.

A report from a young man who spent an exchange term at Choate School in America [25]: "I recommend this school to anyone interested in an exchange, precisely because it is so different from Salem. Sport plays a big role in every American school. The varsity teams serve as the school's advertisement to colleges and universities.The best athletes are concentrated in these varsity teams. The success of the Choate 'Blue and Gold' teams in competition with other New England prep schools determines the status and prestige not only of Choate but also of the individual team members. In my case many were surprised that I did not play soccer, which they thought of as a matter of course for a German."

An account of a Salem girls' hockey team's visit to Gordonstoun School in 1990 [37]: " We were astonished to find that Gordonstoun consists of many buildings widely separated over a vast area, like a real village. We were enthralled by the beautiful Scottish countryside and were delighted to learn 'Original Scottish Dancing.' We lost three of the four hockey matches and tied one—our opponents were just better. Scotland and Gordonstoun impressed me. Was it the school uniform, the more severe discipline, the larger student body, the weathered old buildings, or the Scottish landscape? The ideas of Kurt Hahn about tolerance, and commitment to the welfare of the community, seemed more alive than with us at Salem. It seemed to me, after this short visit, that there was a better sense of community among the students at Gordonstoun; each accepts the others, and lets them be as they are."

And a return visit to Hohenfels the same year by a group of girls from Rannoch school, an affiliate of Gordonstoun [37]: " Morning run at 6:30? What on earth was this Kurt Hahn fellow thinking of? The one real criticism was that some rules are outdated and petty.... Environment felt a lot more relaxed and politer than Rannoch, where both students and staff are under constant pressure to achieve. At Hohenfels the pupils sit attentively through lessons as opposed to their counterparts who are more likely to shout even the more competent teachers down. One aspect we could not get used to was that the teachers sit with the pupils to maintain a degree of order at mealtime. Mealtimes back in Scotland are hurried and riotous.... It was also commented that one could do what one believed in here at Hohenfels without the other pupils making fun. The example of a Chinese boy sitting in his room meditating was given, since such a person would probably have felt ostracized at Rannoch and considered strange."

Finally an excerpt from the valedictorian who spoke on elitism at the Salem graduation ceremonies in 1992 [46]: "Whenever I found myself with others my age and talk turned to 'my' school, the usual response was: 'What? You go to that snobbish school?' Many even reasured me in a friendly way that it did not appear to have affected me. I discovered that an impression was widely shared that Salem is exclusive and harbours correspondingly haughty students." The young lady spoke at some length but seemed to progress no further.

Today both Salem and Gordonstoun are considered elite schools. I don't doubt that superior scholastic aptitude influences selection of students. But for the general public the term is more likely to conjure, with disaproval, superior parental wealth or aristocratic lineage or personal qualities associated with an idealized image of the latter. The elitist image has probably evolved during the many decades that have passed since Hahn's retirement as founding director of the schools. One must remember that after Hahn's arrest at the moment of Salem's greatest peril, he wrote from exile that he would rather the school shut down than reduce the number of scholarship students drawn from the least elite classes. Later at Gordonstoun he welcomed working-class applicants, even though scholastically unprepared, and did not discourage them if they planned to follow their father's manual craft. Still later, when he conceived and created the Outward Bound Schools and the Award Program, his concern had shifted entirely to the education and personal development of all youth. Today nearly 4 million have enrolled in these programs, and countless other millions have been affected indirectly.

But, more comfortable with England's gentlemen than with its commoners, Hahn's personal contact with youth, and hands on experience, was confined to the two boarding schools. Aristocracy, he often said, was the salt that was indispensable to Democracy. Hahn explicitly acknowledged his debt to Plato, and to this philosopher's assertion that the task of education was to select the future leaders, and train them for leadership. From the earliest years at Salem some students felt oppressed by being burdened with this future responsibility.

Now I am persuaded by Popper (*The Open Society and its Enemies*) that Plato's conception has "utterly corrupted the practice of education" (a fascinating account of Plato's program carried to extremes in a tiny African republic appeared in the *New Yorker* for 16 December 1991). Further, I have never been exposed to circles of any elite, and would certainly have been a Social Democrat in Weimar Germany. Why then, and since in any case I am not an educator, did I start to write this book? Five years have passed, and I stretch the truth only a little if I allow myself to say I have forgotten. It was only later, after I had begun to probe into the story, that my real enthusiasm for telling it emerged. Popper suggests what made this story so appealing to record, with this postscript to his criticism: "I do not know a better argument for an optimistic view of mankind than the fact that [Plato's] devastating system has not utterly ruined our secondary schools."

Perhaps it is most of all just this, an optimistic view of mankind and its future, so desperately needed, that the example of this wonderfully benevolent man and his educational innovations has bestowed on us.

APPENDIX

Expeditionary Learning Design Principles

1. THE PRIMACY OF SELF-DISCOVERY
   Learning happens best with emotion, challenge and the requisite support. People discover their abilities, values, "grand passions," and responsibilities in situations that offer adventure and the unexpected. They must have tasks that require perseverance, fitness, craftsmanship, imagination self-discipline and significant achievement. A primary job of the educator is to help students overcome their fear and discover they have more in them than they think.

2. THE HAVING OF WONDERFUL IDEAS
   Teach so as to build on children's curiosity about the world by creating learning situations that provide matter to think about, time to experiment, and time to make sense of what is observed. Foster a community where students' and adults' ideas are respected.

3. THE RESPONSIBILITY FOR LEARNING
   Learning is both a personal, individually specific process of discovery and a social activity. Each of us learns within and for ourselves and as a part of a group. Every aspect of a school must encourage children, young people, and adults to become increasingly responsible for directing their own personal and collective learning.

4. INTIMACY AND CARING
   Learning is fostered best in small groups where there is trust, sustained caring and mutual respect among all members of the learning community. Keep schools and learning groups small. Be sure there is a caring adult looking after the progress of each child. Arrange for the older students to mentor the younger ones.

5. SUCCESS AND FAILURE
   All students must be assured a fair measure of success in learning in order to nurture the confidence and capacity to take risks and rise to increasingly difficult challenges. But it is also important to experience failure, to overcome negative inclinations, to prevail against adversity and to learn to turn disabilities into opportunities.

6. COLLABORATION AND COMPETITION
   Teach so as to join individual and group development so that the value of friendship, trust, and group endeavor is made manifest. Encourage students to compete, not against each other, but with their own personal best and with rigorous standards of excellence.

7. DIVERSITY AND INCLUSIVITY
   Diversity and inclusivity in all groups dramatically increases richness of ideas, creative power, problem-solving ability, and acceptance of others. Encourage students to investigate, value and draw upon their own different histories, talents and resources together with those of other communities and cultures. Keep the schools and learning groups heterogeneous.

8. THE NATURAL WORLD
   A direct and respectful relationship with the natural world refreshes the human spirit and reveals the important lessons of recurring cycles and cause and effect. Students learn to become stewards of the earth and of the generations to come.

9. SOLITUDE AND REFLECTION
   Solitude, reflection and silence replenish our energies and open our minds. Be sure students have time alone to explore their own thoughts, make their own connections and create their own ideas. Then give them opportunity to exchange their reflections with each other and with adults.

10. SERVICE AND COMPASSION
   We are crew, not passengers, and are strengthened by acts of consequential service to others. One of a school's primary functions is to prepare its students with the attitudes and skills to learn from and be of service to others.

REFERENCES

Recent or accessible books are cited in the text. References listed here are to unpublished material, or to publications that are out of print or probably not readily available in libraries. Some of the documents from which I have quoted excerpts are reprinted in full in a recent scholarly work dealing with the Salem schools (Ref. 9).

1. *Kurt Hahn*, Edited by by H. Röhrs and H. Tunstall-Behrens, 1970, Routledge and Kegan Paul, London.

2. "Der Fall Potempa," by P. Kluke, *Vierteljahreshefte für Zeitgeschickte* 5, 279 (1957).

3. Kurt Hahn Archives, Schule Schloss Salem, 88682 Salem, Germany.

4. *Kurt Hahn: an Appreciation of his Life and Work*, compiled by D.A. Byatt, 1976, Published by Gordonstoun School, University Press, Aberdeen.

5. Mitteilungen der Altsalemer Vereinigung, December 1990.

6. "Outward Bound": Address by Kurt Hahn at the Annual Meeting of the Outward Bound Trust on 20th July, 1960. Issued by the Outward Bound Trust, 123 Victoria St. SW1, London.

7. Jocelin Winthrop-Young, Memoir of 1986, K. H. Archives, Schule Schloss Salem.

8. "An Experiment in Education" by Kurt Hahn. *The Listener,* November 16, 1950.

9. *Werte und Wege der Erlebnispädigogik Schule Schloss Salem,* by Anja Pielorz, 1991, Hermann Luchterhand Verlag.

10. *Festreden und Ansprachen: 80th Geburtstag Kurt Hahn*. Publisher: A. Holzschuh, Ravensburg, Germany.

11. "A German Public School" by Kurt Hahn. *The Listener*, January 17, 1934.

12. *Gordonstoun: Ancient Estate and Modern School*, by Henry L. Brereton, 1968, W. and A. Chambers Ltd., London.

13. *Reminiscences and Reflections: a Youth in Germany*, by Golo Mann, 1990, W. W. Norton and Co., New York.

14. Wilhelm Kuchenmüller, Memoir of 1981, K. H. Archives, Schule Schloss Salem.

15. *Kurt Hahn: Erziehung und die Krise der Demokratie*, Edited by Michael Knoll, 1986, Stuttgart: Klett-Cotta.

16. "The Struggle of Salem School against the Nazi Regime," an address by Erich Meissner to the Gordonstoun Society, January 1942, Archives, Gordonstoun School, Elgin, Morayshire IV3 2 RF, Great Britain.

17. *Unfolding Character: The Impact of Gordonstoun*, by Adam Arnold-Brown, 1962, Routledge and Kegan Paul.

18. *Outward Bound U.S.A.*, by Joshua L. Miner and Joe Boldt, 1981, William Morrow and Co. Inc.

19. *Die Deutschen Kurzschulen*, by Helga Weber and Jörg Ziegenspeck, 1983, Beltz Verlag.

20. *Die Kurzschulen Kurt Hahn's,* by Karl Schwarz, 1968, A. Henn Verlag, Ratingen bei Düsseldorf.

21. *Challenge: The Duke of Edinburgh's Award in Action*, Edited by Peter Carpenter, 1966, Ward Lock & Co., Ltd.

22. *The Trevelyan Scholarships*, by Ronald Peddie, 1975, the Roundwood Press.

23. *Schools Across Frontiers: The Story of the International Baccalaureate and the United World Colleges*, by A.D.C. Peterson, 1987, Open Court Press.

24. "Chroniken der Schule Spetzgart", Anonymous, 1932-3, K. H. Archives,

25. Salemerhefte, Vol. 55, 1982-84.

26. Hildegard Disch, *Die Schule Schloss Salem in den Jahren 1933-1945.* Schule Schloss Salem Sonderheft 28, 1949.

27. *Schlaglichter aus der Unbruchzeit* (Nazi-Zeit), Anonymous, 1933, K. H. Archives, Schule Schloss Salem.

28. Fraulein Casek, Diary, 1933, K. H. Archives, Schule Schloss Salem.

29. *Exeter Studies in History* : Vol. I, No. 6, Chapters 4-5, 1983; Vol. II, No. 8, Chapter 19, 1984. Editors: J. Noakes and G. Pridham, Published by the University of Exeter.

30. Marina Ewald, "Diary from the installation of the Kommisar until my departure," 1933, K. H. Archives, Schule Schloss Salem.

31. Letter of 19 June 1933, von Brauchitsch to Hitler. K. H. Archives, Schule Schloss Salem.

32. Letter of 22 September 1933, Ministerialrat Herbert Kraft to Katharina Arnold-Forster. K. H. Archives, Schule Schloss Salem.

33. M. M. Forell, "Salemer Bericht, Autumn 1934 to Easter 1936," K. H. Archives, Schule Schloss Salem.

34. Address by Ministerialrat Kraft, 25 July 1933, at Salem. K. H. Archives, Schule Schloss Salem.

35. Address by Professor Mittelstrass, 25 July 1933, at Salem. K. H. Archives, Schule Schloss Salem.

36. J.W.Y., Biographical Sketch of Fräulein Ewald, March 1973, K. H. Archives, Schule Schloss Salem.

37. Salemerhefte, Vol. 58, 1990-1991.

38. "Philip Mountbatten," Press Release written by Kurt Hahn at the time of Prince Philip's engagement to Princess Elizabeth. K.H. Archives, Schule Schloss Salem.

39 *Kurt Hahn: Errinerungen—Gedanken—Aufforderungen. Beiträge zum 100. Geburtstag des Reformpädagogen*, 1987. Publisher: Verlag Klaus Neubauer, Lüneburg.

40. Letter of 10 October 1934, Fritz Fellner to Markgraf Berthold. K. H. Archives, Schule Schloss Salem.

41. Letter of 7 October, 1937, Ministerialrat Kraft to Party Headquarters in Munich. K. H. Archives, Schule Schloss Salem.

42. Letter of 1 January 1944, H. Blendinger to the Salem school body. K. H. Archives, Schule Schloss Salem.

43. Mitteilungen der Altsalemer Vereinigung, April 1993.

44. *Bildung als Wagnis und Bewährung*, Edited by Hermann Röhrs,1966, Quelle and Meyer, Heidelberg.

45. Mitteilungen der Altsalemer Vereinigung, April 1989.

46. *Das Magazin*, December 1992, a new Salem alumni newsletter.

INDEX